forcing, etc

ing, etc

the indoor gardener's guide
to bringing bulbs, branches,
& houseplants into bloom

by KATHERINE WHITESIDE

with photographs by RICHARD FELBER

WORKMAN PUBLISHING · NEW YORK

Library of Congress Cataloging-in-Publication Data
Whiteside, Katherine. 1952-
Forcing, etc: the indoor gardener's guide to bringing bulbs, branches,
and houseplants into bloom / by Katherine Whiteside.
p. cm.
ISBN 0-7611-1512-9
1. Forcing (Plants). 2. Indoor gardening. I. Title.
SB414.W55 1999
635.9'82—dc21   99-32784
 CIP

Workman Publishing Company
708 Broadway, New York, NY 10003-9555

Manufactured in Italy

First printing October 1999
10 9 8 7 6 5 4 3 2 1

Special thanks to

HELEN ANDERSON
RENÉE BEAULIEU
VICTOR CARLSON
PAGE DICKEY
JANIS DONNAUD
RICHARD FELBER
PETER GERGELY
PAUL HANSON
ELIZABETH JOHNSBOEN
SALLY KOVALCHICK
JOHN MEILS
DIANE PHILLIPS
RITA RIEHLE
TONY SKITTONE
MARY WILKINSON
PETER WORKMAN

This book is dedicated to

DEAN ANDERSON

MICAH HALES

AUGUST HALES

CONTENTS

INTRODUCTION indoors: bulbs, blossoms, and branches

AN AMATEUR'S GUIDE TO INDOOR PLANTS

The urge to grow plants is as basic as the homing instinct, and anyone with a window and a wish can garden indoors. Too many people deny themselves the pleasure of plants because they live in an apartment and don't have a garden, or because they do have a garden and it's buried in snow half the year. In either case, you'll soon discover how easily a sunny-faced crocus, a tiny forest of ferns, a gigantic calla lily, or even a vaseful of peach blossoms will forever put to rest the idea that many plants are simply too much work. The well-considered indoor plant is not just another mute piece of furniture. Great plants—whether large or small, in groups or single—are lively objets d'art bearing a joyous

✺ LEFT A spiky agave and a shrubby hebe from the garden add to the indoor winter scene. The garden table is set with the tender bulb Scilla peruviana and forced corylopsis branches.

message that comes across more clearly than the welcome on your doormat.

Here you'll discover that bulbs offer a fascinating introduction to the mysteries of gardening. At first glance, a bag of tulip bulbs seems as unpromising as a sack of pebbles. Packed inside the brown hardness of each sleeping bulb, however, is the possibility of green leaves and a brightly colored flower or two. The trick is to figure out how to get those leaves and flowers to come out of that little treasure chest, and an even greater feat is to persuade that bulb to pop open indoors. Thankfully, these techniques were figured out long ago and enthusiastically passed from one generation to another, so this winter you, too, can experience tulips blooming on your table when the snow is building up. Forcing bulbs is magic—but it's the kind of magic anyone can make.

∾ LEFT *A forced* Tulipa *'Oscar,' a miniature rose 'Fame Parade,' and a spicy red dianthus create an indoor Valentine greeting in February.*

Another kind of magic happens indoors when bulbs from another hemisphere "think" that summer has arrived. Tender bulbs from the Southern Hemisphere have the opposite growing season from Northern Hemisphere bulbs. Southern Hemisphere bulbs are naturally programmed so that December marks their spring growing season, and their peak summer-flowering moment occurs in March. All you have to do is help that bulb—now far from home—keep its upside-down schedule intact. Observing an enormous calla lily unroll fragrant flower after flower while cold winds howl outdoors is an enchantment open to anyone who gardens indoors.

As pots of bulbs placed around the house mark the passing of winter, you may further embellish your environment with other indoor treats such as glorious plants and flowering branches. Fragrant jasmine is an easy pleasure, crisp-leaved ivy is faithful even in the darkest apartment, and a potted rosemary can be constantly plucked to add a taste of sun to simmering stews. Additionally, woods, fields, and even most backyards have at least a few winter-bare twigs that can be cut and coaxed into springlike blooms and leaves. Finally, when the days get longer, your indoor garden can expand, too. Cuttings, divisions, and baby plants become as much a part of spring as the first birdsong, and before you turn around, you've had an entire season of gardening without setting a foot outdoors. Surely, that is magic.

You don't need lots of fancy stuff to grow wonderful plants. When you begin on a small scale and are determined to conquer the basics, there is little initial outlay for equipment. Indoor gardening takes place right in your home, so you really don't need to run around buying big forcing lights, bushels of potting soil, boxes of plastic pots, and hundreds of different tools. It's far better to pick out plants that will thrive in your existing light levels, and to match

these with pretty pots as you need them. Except for rare occasions, you're not going to need enormous quantities of soil or tools on hand, so buy what you need when you need it. A simple start almost always assures future success, and making wise choices significantly ups the ante.

WHAT YOU DON'T NEED

To grow great plants, you definitely don't need a greenhouse, but you do need a window. In subsequent chapters, you'll discover that even a sunny window isn't necessary—many plants are as susceptible to sunburn as a redhead on a beach. If you decide to get involved with plants that require artificial lights, you may enjoy creating your own setup. However, if rigging and

wiring doesn't appeal to you, don't fret. None of the plants in this book were raised under grow lights (although some were purchased from a greenhouse).

When it comes to tools, the population of the world divides into two basic groups. Half

≈ LEFT *Designer Page Dickey's indoor garden defies wintertime blues.* ≈ RIGHT *A fat green bulb of* Ornithogalum caudatum *(commonly known as pregnant onion) shares an antique pot with a crispy-leaved ivy.*

the people cherish, protect, oil, and honor their well-sharpened, expensive clippers. The others buy cheap—and often—because their clippers suffer the crippling effects of cutting across wires, sawing through sand-coated plastic pots, and countless other ruinous practices. A collection of small-scale indoor gardening tools can be a beautiful addition to your garden tableau, but an old wooden spoon, a pair of scissors, and some ancient Tupperware mixing bowls kept under the sink right next to your ratty plastic watering can will do the job just fine.

WHAT YOU DO NEED

When it comes to indoor plant cultivation, there is only one absolute essential: that you grow the right plant in the right place. A cool, dark apart-

∾ LEFT *Offspring of the pregnant onion* (Ornithogalum caudatum) *were plucked from the mother bulb and given their own pot.*

ment is perfect for growing certain types of ferns, orchids, and bulbs. A hot, dry house begs for a crazy cactus collection, a shelfful of succulents, or a lovely little lime tree. If you live in a highrise in Los Angeles, forcing daffodils and tulips is probably a waste of your time and refrigerator space, but growing a statuesque veltheimia would beautifully suit your warm Pacific-rim habitat. Likewise, a drafty farmhouse in wintry New Hampshire is no happy home for tender tropical bulbs, but an indoor show of hardy hyacinths will keep your spirits up through the most snowy February. Plants cannot be persuaded to rise above a series of ill-conceived whims. They are living things that respond to repeated insults like any other living thing—first they pout, next they suffer, then they go away.

ఞ RIGHT *Pelargoniums, commonly known as geraniums, make happy houseplants. Grow either the common garden varieties or the old-fashioned scented types.*

EASY DOES IT

Plant cultivation is not difficult if you follow the path of least resistance. Once you pick the right plant, your success is just about guaranteed. Use

a notebook to scribble down instructions on fertilizing and watering requirements, or better yet, jot the information on a calendar. Life is known to get hectic just when you least expect it to. You may need to delegate plant tending once in a while, and if the information needed to get the job done is handy, there's much less stress involved.

The world of indoor gardening is enormous, and the scope of this book is small. But even the briefest glance at the following five chapters should convince you that this is the time to begin a little indoor garden. You can start with forcing hardy bulbs like crocuses and tulips to cheer you through long and cold winters, or you may consider the cultivation of tender bulbs as a reminder that cold winters are only a matter of where you land. Tapping into the inherent creativity that bonds even a hard-scrabble farmer to his beautifully tidy vegetable garden, you'll find it impossible to grow a plant well and not wonder at the miracle that connects people to plants. It's a hard heart that denies all the sweetness of jasmine festooning a kitchen window, and a sad day when no forsythia branches on the piano play fortune teller with promises of spring. The thin strings of roots that first appear in your own jar of coleus cuttings will tug at your heart. It doesn't take long for the beginner to realize that a simple plant is much more than pretty blossoms and handsome leaves.

∾ LEFT *A peaceful northern window is decorated with forced apple branches, a pot of snowdrops, and a recently divided clump of lemongrass resting under an inverted glass vase.*

CHAPTER ONE hardy bulbs: the forced

GETTING A HANDLE ON HARDY BULBS

HARDY BULBS are the agreeable, cold-loving, easy-to-grow flowers of the spring garden. Native to the temperate zones of the world, these bulbs can also be coaxed into bloom indoors. This group includes crocuses, hyacinths, and daffodils, as well as snowdrops, scillas, tulips, irises, and any other spring-flowering bulbs that burst into col-orful life outdoors after a cold winter of freezing temperatures.

In horticulture, "hardy" is an imprecise term that refers to a plant's (in this case a bulb's) ability to survive year-round outdoors. But a Thompson and Morgan catalog from England will confidently assure you that plant is hardy

∾ LEFT *This indoor garden table is filled with February's forced hardy bulbs. Three types of narcissus, both yellow species and purple hybrid irises, tulips, eranthis, puschkinia, and muscari create a cheerful welcome.*

when it won't survive a New York minute outside on a normal New England winter's day. Many bulbs that do very well outdoors in Louisiana—bursting into bloom on the February lawn—will not survive the cold winters on a Maine lawn. And for the gardener in Miami, an amaryllis may live through the year outdoors and thus be considered hardy there, yet it's not hardy for the gardener who lives in Chicago.

Half the joy of growing plants, however, is realizing that imprecision is not going to doom you to failure. Even a stark-raving amateur can magically coax pots and pots of cute little crocuses, sweetly scented hyacinths, and cheerful daffodils to bloom indoors while three feet of snow blankets the world outside.

When growing bulbs indoors where temperature, light, and water are controlled by the gardener, the term "hardy bulb" has a different connotation. Hardy bulbs, which grow naturally in colder parts of the world—such as the mountains of China, Russia, and the temperate zones of Europe—actually *require* this cold-winter period or they will not bloom. When growing hardy bulbs indoors, the colder climate is supplied by the gardener, either by keeping pots

∾ LEFT *The double early* Tulipa *'Mr. Van Der Hoef'— an excellent choice for forcing—was first bred in 1911.*

of bulbs outside in cold weather, or by artificially chilling the bulbs. Providing this faux winter is part of the process of forcing.

Before describing the magical ways in which hardy bulbs can be urged into early bloom indoors, it must be mentioned that even the word "bulb" is ambiguous. *Hortus Third,* the beloved brown bible for many American gardeners, determines that "when defined as a horticultural class, bulbs are ornamental, partial season, mostly simple-stemmed plants arising from bulbs, corms, tubers, or thickened rhizomes." *Hortus* adds that "the term [bulb] is used more loosely and imprecisely in horticulture than in botany." There has, however, been a movement by those who adore precision to replace the loosely rattling collective noun "bulb" (which *Hortus* says *is* acceptable to use) with the more

scientific term "geophyte." But regular, just-for-pleasure gardeners associate the term "bulb" with a group of plants that, after a period of blooming and making leaves, goes dormant and retreats back into a solid little nugget that stores a sleeping yet viable plant. "Bulb" is the word that has been used for eons to describe that little

∾ RIGHT *After four months, emerging leaves from* Tulipa *'Fire Queen' indicated that it was ready to be moved from its cold, dark spot to a chilly, light position.*

"True" Bulbs, Tubers, Rhizomes, and Corms Are All Bulbs

Although gardeners say that tulips, narcissus, crocuses, lilies, and irises are all "bulbs," botanists differentiate between what they call "true" bulbs, tubers, rhizomes, and corms.

The familiar cooking onion is a true bulb, as is the tulip, daffodil, and hyacinth. True bulbs contain a stem and leaves nestled inside in tightly packed layers. True bulbs usually have a pointy top and a flat bottom; and in the case of tulips, one side is slightly flat, too.

Tubers also belong to the bulbous group of plants. Unlike true bulbs, they do not contain layers of leaves because tubers are specialized underground stems that serve as storage organs. Potatoes are actually tubers; dahlias and certain types of begonias are flowering tubers.

Rhizomes are also underground stems modified for storage, and they do not contain layers of leaves. The fresh ginger root used in cooking is a rhizome. The rhizome most familiar to gardeners is the German (or "bearded") iris, but the tender South African calla lily also grows from a large rhizome.

A corm is also a swollen underground stem (without packed leaves) that serves as a storage organ. Corms are roundish and flattened on top, and have slightly indented bottoms. Crocuses (at left) come from corms.

Don't be afraid to call true bulbs, tubers, rhizomes, and corms by the simple catchall term "bulbs." All catalogs do.

treasure chest packed with quiescent leaves and a flower, and it's safe to predict that the term will not soon be replaced.

THE GENTLE ART OF PERSUASION

In the outdoor hardy bulb world, corms, tubers, thickened rhizomes, and true bulbs are purchased and buried outside in autumn when the air temperature begins to drop. Soon after they are planted, the basal plate (bottom) of the bulb sprouts roots deep into the still-warm soil. The cooler surface air prevents the leaves and flowers from hastily sprouting upward toward sure death. Next—and this is where the word *hardy* comes into play—these bulbs must go through a specific period of cold weather (winter) to rest and prepare for upcoming events. When the

longer days and warmer temperatures of spring finally arrive, each bulb slowly cracks open. A green shoot appears, and shortly after, amazing flowers start to unfold like brightly colored

∾ RIGHT *A warm day in mid October is the perfect time for potting up bulbs.*

banners being pulled from a box. It's a miracle that never fails to thrill.

Weather has some bearing on when your garden-planted bulbs will bloom, but you can count on snowdrops and crocuses to show up first, followed by waves of narcissus (in catalogs, growers specify early-season, mid-season, and late-season), with the familiar tulip family generally popping up sometime later in the spring.

Ingeniously, generations of gardeners have learned to circumvent the outdoor requirements of growing hardy bulbs. The ancient Romans figured out how to dig up native bulbs that flourished on the Italian hillsides and encourage them to bloom indoors. The indomitable Philip Miller, who ran London's Chelsea Physic Garden for the better part of the 1700s, delighted in forcing bulbs indoors.

ᔍ LEFT *Crocus vernus 'Vanguard' has three outside petals of silvery-blue that open to reveal inner petals of bright purple.*

But it was the domestically inclined Victorians who brought the gentle art of forcing hardy bulbs to the masses, and for them—in the times before central heating, huge glass windows, and indoor water faucets—growing bulbs indoors was pursued as edifying entertainment. By 1832, a nursery run by the Landreth family offered 50 different varieties of hyacinths for sale, almost all of them destined to serve indoors as the Victorian equivalent of the modern sitcom. Although today it might be difficult to find (and redundant to grow) 50 different hyacinths, the scope of Victorian-era availability signaled that forcing hardy bulbs indoors was then a widely practiced activity.

Perhaps this year you, too, can join in the great tradition of jump-starting spring with forced bulbs. By beginning in autumn, you can

coax pots of charming, out-of-season flowers into later bloom and recreate a suitably arcane way to triumph over winter's doldrums.

Forcing. Although the technique of getting hardy bulbs to bloom indoors is called forcing, anybody who enjoys this activity year after year will tell you that coaxing, cajoling, and down-

∾ RIGHT *A quick and easy way to satisfy your most harried gardening urges is to repot inexpensive, store-bought forced tulips.*

right humoring describes the process more clearly. You can "force" a bulb only so far—outside certain parameters, it is simply going to keep its little lid slammed shut and refuse to grow.

There's nothing really difficult, however, about getting hardy bulbs to grow indoors. The process is as simple as a three-step recipe, and although we are stuck with calling it forcing, it is truly an easy, beautiful, and gentle art. All you have to do is simulate late autumn, deep winter, and early spring in an accelerated time frame.

After mentioning speed and time, it's interesting to note that forcing bulbs fell out of general favor during the hectic years of the last part of the twentieth century. Fault for this may lie squarely on the shoulders of those who decreed that the December holiday season—which already featured lots of cooking, feasting, entertaining at home, going out to parties, decorating, cleaning, gift-gathering, present-presenting,

and all-around endless schlepping—was somehow incomplete without forced bulbs thrown into the mix. Overkill on pushing bulb forcing as yet another holiday obligation just about put this quiet little activity into its grave.

∾ LEFT *Acting as one column in winter's forced-hyacinth parade, 'Distinction' perches on the top ledge, 'City of Haarlem' glows in a green vase, 'Carnegie' dazzles in a brass container, and 'Gipsy Queen' poses in a swirled gold jug.*
∾ ABOVE *An assortment of chilling pots feature (from left to right) the fat tulip leaves of 'Queen of the Night,' Iris* cristata, *and lily of the valley.*

This year, consider delaying the forcing process so that flowering begins after the bustle of the holidays is over and your household has returned to its own peaceful routines. Then a succession of wintertime blooms will truly delight—and you, your family, and your visitors will have time to enjoy all the surprising colors and scents offered up by your hardy bulbs.

In January, February, and March you can revel in beautiful bulbs such as 'Gipsy Girl' crocuses, 'Orange Queen' narcissus, and 'King of the Blues' hyacinths without the distraction of glitter and gift wrappings. These first months of the new year can mark a quiet time when an invitation for tea—and a flower-admiration moment—is a real treat to help bridge the long winter months before spring.

∾ LEFT *The antique hyacinth 'Gipsy Queen' (originally bred in 1927) is an unusual apricot color and has a very pleasant, fruity perfume. This water-forced bulb stayed in full bloom for more than twenty days.*

When to Call About Your Bulbs

When you open your bags of bulbs, there should be no unpleasant odors signifying rot. The bulbs should be dry and should not feel squishy. Sometimes a few specks of mold may appear on some bulbs, but unless the bulb is positively rotten, it will flower just fine.

Some narcissus and crocus bulbs may have tiny sprouts coming from them. Be careful not to break these off because this is the beginning of the plant. If the sprouts are long (longer than two inches for narcissus, or one inch for crocuses), call the catalog company to make sure that the bulbs can be expected to flower. Improper storage at warm temperatures causes bulbs to sprout prematurely and may compromise their blooming.

Bulbs (such as the puschkinias at right) need to be stored away from heat,

moisture, and light. Leave them in their original bags and boxes. A cool basement or garage can provide good spots for storage, but don't put bulbs anywhere near fruit, which emits a gas that makes bulbs produce deformed flowers.

A great way to store your bulbs is in those old cookie tins that you simply couldn't bear to throw away. Leave the bulbs in their paper bags, but place them inside the tins, then label and store them at the proper temperature. No critter could possibly breach a metal mini-fortress, and as a bonus, your hoarding instincts will be forever validated.

PROVENANCE COUNTS

Advice for purchasing hardy bulbs hasn't changed a bit since the Victorian era. *Henderson's Bulb Culture,* published in 1904, implored read-

ers to "BUY THE BEST!" and this simple statement remains true. Although there are bargains to be had in the garden world, when it comes to bulbs, you generally get what you pay for. For this reason, mail-order catalogs with familiar names, big reputations, and generations of experience are where to put your bulb money. People whose livelihoods rest in supplying great bulbs will make sure that the ones they send you are disease free and have been stored at the proper temperatures. And if something on their end goes wrong, they'll go out of their way to make it up to you. Catalogs offer huge selections and great prices, and are hard to beat in the bulb department (see the Resource Guide on page 151).

With catalogs, the selection of bulbs suitable for forcing is large and designated.

〜 LEFT *The delicate* Narcissus *'Orange Queen,' an antique bulb dating back to 1908, is hardy in zones six through eight and is very easy to force indoors.*

B u l b   P r i m e r

HYACINTH

For the totally inexperienced indoor gardener, hyacinths are probably the easiest bulbs to force. This has been true at least since 1873, when Henry T. Williams wrote in *Window Gardening* that hyacinths were the most popular for forcing "simply because greater variety of color and quantity of bloom can be had for less trouble and expense than any other." These bulbs can be forced in pots of soil or in water (see "Water Forcing" on page 44), and they rarely disappoint.

Often you will see forced hyacinths available for purchase almost at the point of bloom. These are usually the rose-pink variety called 'Pink Pearl' (bred in 1922) or the pure white 'Carnegie' (1935). Both have a vibrant fragrance. (Hyacinths are famous for their sweet scents—two hyacinths in full bloom amply perfume a large room, and where three or more are gathered, you may run

the risk of putting your more delicate guests off their meal.)

You can safely order lesser-known varieties of hyacinth and still expect rousing success. 'Distinction' (above) bred in 1880, has beautiful pickled-beet-colored blossoms and dark maroon stems that, when water-forced, complement the wine-colored bulb. 'City of Haarlem'

(1893) is a gentle pale yellow color, and 'King of the Blues' (1863) has loose flowers and a subtle perfume. (If you're into color combinations, these two are beautiful when paired on a cool windowsill.) The pale lilac 'Splendid Cornelia' is gorgeous, and 'Gipsy Queen' is a heart-stopping pale apricot; like the others mentioned, they keep their bloom for quite a while if placed in a cool location. For a slightly different look in hyacinths, try looser-flowered, multi-stemmed blue 'Borah.'

For forcing in soil, hyacinths should be potted up by mid October. Use ordinary potting medium, and for best effect, place bulbs close together but not touching. The pointy tops of the bulbs should be about half an inch above the soil line. Water the bulbs thoroughly, and place the pots in a cold (35° to 48°F), dark location for at least twelve weeks. If the bulbs start to heave up out of the soil during rooting, add a layer of gravel on top to weigh them down a bit, taking care not to cover the pointy tops. Keep the plants watered and in the dark until bulb shoots reach one inch tall. At this point, move the pot to a cool (55°F), light location (a north-facing window is perfect).

Almost all catalogs now offer "top-size" bulbs and less expensive "landscape-size." Top-size bulbs are the largest available, and each bulb is fully mature and ready to produce a bumper crop of blooms. Landscape-size bulbs are smaller and less mature, and require several seasons of garden growth to achieve peak blooming capacity. Always buy top-size bulbs for forcing.

Also pay attention to how the catalog copy describes certain bulbs. The best bulbs for forcing are early bloomers with strong, shortish stems. Bulbs that bloom early outside bloom even earlier inside, and with the lower light levels indoors, long stems tend to become weak and lanky. For example, the long-stemmed "French" tulips that look so elegant in florists' arrangements are not good candidates for forcing because, under the conditions provided by an amateur grower, those stems will unnaturally elongate (even further) and the poor tulip will not be able to hold its head up. Your best bets for forcing are tulips with stems a foot tall or less. A good rule of thumb is to follow the catalog's

∞ LEFT *There's nothing better to cheer up a late February morning than crocus buds opening on the breakfast table.*
∞ RIGHT Narcissus *'Tête à Tête,'* pale Crocus *'Snow-bunting,'* and purple Crocus *'Remembrance'* decorate an entryway garden table.

B u l b   P r i m e r

CROCUS

Although some people may overlook crocuses in the garden, when forced in small pots or singly in water, they create a stir all out of proportion to their little size. Crocuses are usually divided into three groups, and members from each group are suitable for forcing. *Crocus chrysanthus* varieties bloom first, then the larger-flowered *C. vernus* types, and finally species such as *C. angustifolius* and *C. tomasinianus* chime in on their own schedules.

As a rule, crocus flowers do not last as long indoors as hyacinths, but keeping them cool and out of sunny windows will extend their bloom. Also, because many crocus varieties produce another flower after the first one fades, be sure to deadhead (remove spent blooms), using a baby's nail scissors to avoid smashing the teeny stems.

The two crocuses that you can usually purchase already forced are the purple *C. vernus* 'Remembrance' and the white-and-

purple-striped 'Pickwick.' Also from this group is the lesser known 'Vanguard,' with its three pewter and three pale purple petals—a knockout when it unfurls each morning.

Other surefire favorites from the *C. chrysanthus* group include the sweetly scented pure white 'Snowbunting' (1914) and the saucy little 'Gipsy Girl' (at left), who truly flicks her petticoats at you. 'Moonlight' (1924) was one of Vita Sackville-West's pets at Sissinghurst; *C. tomasinianus* (1847) is the beloved little "Tommy" of old Southern gardens.

When you begin planting your crocuses, remember that their small flowers look better and more in proportion in a small pot. Using mid October as your big potting-up day, place at least ten crocus corms closely together in a six-inch pot. Use ordinary potting soil with a bit of sand added to insure quick drainage. Cover the corms with one inch of soil and pat down firmly. Water, and place the pot in a cold, dark place (35° to 48°F) for about eleven weeks. Water frequently so the soil remains moist to the touch.

Crocuses make favorite snacks for mice, so be sure that your storage area is secure. When chilling is complete and shoots appear, move to a cool (55°F), light area, such as near a north-facing window. In about two and a half weeks, small, tear-shaped buds will appear in the foliage. Keep watered, and flowers will bloom within several days.

recommendations for forcing bulbs until you gain your sea legs after a couple of seasons. After that, let it rip and try anything your heart desires.

Bulb catalogs start arriving as early as June, and although it's hard to think of winter right then, do mull over what you want before autumn arrives. Some catalogs specialize in heirloom bulbs, others have Dutch names, and some are as Yankee as picket fences (see the Resource Guide on page 151).

Begin with at least three different catalogs and read through them to familiarize yourself with the basics. Once you've decided on your budget, start circling, noting, and scribbling down your favorite choices. You can put together a lot of forcing material and spend less than $75. A dozen crocuses, a pair of hyacinths, six tulips, and two different kinds of daffodils would disappear in the garden, but for about $40 you can force a dozen scented 'Snowbunting' crocuses, two nineteenth-century

'L'Innocence' hyacinths, six old-fashioned 'Electra' tulips, and two dozen each of 'Rip Van Winkle' and 'Avalanche' daffodils. Some catalogs even offer discounts if you order before Labor Day.

❧ ABOVE *Don't be afraid to let your forced bulbs swoop gracefully. Your indoor garden will appear more natural if you stake only those plants that threaten to topple or break.*

Even when you order early, your bulbs will not arrive until it's time for you to plant. When your bulbs are delivered, open the boxes and make sure that your entire order has arrived. Also, open the individual bags and make sure there's not a lot of mold or sickly yellow sprouts. If either has ocurred, call the company right away and tell them—they'll probably send replacements.

If all is well, store your bulbs in a cool, dry, shaded location until planting day. Certain critters love to munch on bulbs, so be sure to put them in a protected place. Tulips, crocuses, and fritillaries are especially appealing to animals. It's a very sad morning when you discover that raccoons have gone through bags of specially ordered tulip bulbs on the back porch like children gleefully snorting through cookies. Unfortunately, if your bulbs are scoffed down by wildlife, you'll get sympathy from your mail-order company, but no new bulbs.

ॐ LEFT *The truly ancient* Eranthis hyemalis *has been in cultivation since 1578. A very early bloomer outside, these delicate flowers are a treat when forced indoors.*
ॐ RIGHT *These pots of hardy bulbs are receiving their cold treatment in the woodshed. They will be watered every week.*

∾ ABOVE *The new leaves of* Iris cristata *sprout in a cool location. This small iris, a native plant with dove-gray flowers, can be dug from the garden and potted up for forcing.*
∾ RIGHT *The white-and-green-striped leaves of this crocus are pretty even after the flowers have gone.*

BEYOND THE BASICS

Besides the Big Four for forcing (hyacinths, crocuses, narcissus, and tulips), various other little gems also work well on windowsills. The small, bulbous irises are stunning and easy to force. Bright yellow *Iris danfordiae* blooms very early, and one pot makes your house smell like the Philadelphia Flower Show. *I. histrioides* 'George' perches in pots like giant purple-and-green dragonflies ready for takeoff; and *I. reticulata* 'Harmony' is after-the-storm-blue and fragrant. Other small irises for forcing include *I. reticulata* 'Natascha,' a very early blooming off-white variety, and the almost black (actually, very dark blue) *I. r.* 'Pixie.' All of these have stems that reach only about six inches tall, so consider planting them in smaller pots when forcing.

After a season or two of winter-flower success, you will doubtlessly enjoy further forcing adventures. Remember to stick to short-

stemmed early bloomers, and simply peruse your catalogs to see what fits those requirements. *Scilla siberica* is an intense medium blue color, and the small bulbs can be individually forced in very small pots. An uncommon but very easy bulb to grow in pots is *Puschkinia scilloides* var. *libanotica.* This delightful bulb has milky blue

flowers with pencil-thin veins of darker blue; it looks stunning when the pots are shown off on silver trays. Blue or pink chionodoxa are happy forcers and present their broad, cheerful faces to the sun, giving them a well-deserved reputation as sturdy little cottage flowers. The very early blooming winter aconites and snowdrops look sweet in aged terra-cotta pots, and by adding these two to your forcing schedule, you can have flowers from deepest winter all the way (through your other bulbs) into springtime.

THE NARCISSUS QUESTION

Sometimes the classification of plants can be quite confusing. Such is the case with the genus *Narcissus,* which includes the commonly named

∾ LEFT *Move crocus pots from their cold place (40°F) to a chilly spot (50°F) when sprouts are two inches tall.*

daffodils, jonquils, and tazettas, in addition to all the flowers we usually call narcissus. Botanist tried to clarify *Narcissus* nomenclature by dividing this large genus into eleven divisions, according to whether the flowers were Large-Cupped, Small-Cupped, Trumpet, Tazetta, Jonquilla, and so on. Still, when all was said and done, a bunch of leftovers were lumped into division eleven, known as Miscellaneous. Even highly trained specialists couldn't unravel this nomenclature knot. Therefore, the home gardener can relax when it comes to the narcissus question and keep in mind that anything looking vaguely daffodil-ish is probably included in the genus *Narcissus.*

An important fact for the home gardener to know, however, is that not all narcissus are hardy bulbs. Although catalogs commonly list every member of this genus in one section, some narcissus are hardy and require a period of cold to force them into early bloom, while others are tender and require warmth at all times. Both hardy and tender narcissus are easy to coax into winter bloom in your house (refer to "Narcissus" on page 43, and "Paperwhites" on page 38, for the different requirements).

∾ RIGHT *Multi-flowered narcissus bulbs unfurl small bouquets on every stem.*

B u l b   P r i m e r

TULIP

The story of tulipomania, an obsession that gripped the Dutch between 1634 and 1637, could serve as a cautionary tale to crazed Internet investors. The entire Dutch economy went down the tubes during this period from rash, uncontrolled speculation in tulip bulbs that didn't actually exist. John Parkinson had written in 1629 that "there is no lady or gentleman of any worth that is not caught with their delight," but many people soon discovered that their "delight" cost them their fortunes. The lesson is that history inevitably repeats itself, and that tulips are best grown for pure pleasure.

Tulips are a bit tricky to force, but deliver quite a bang for your buck. 'Apricot Beauty' and 'Christmas Marvel' are the standard already-potted varieties, but

recently the gorgeous double yellow 'Monte Carlo' and the cheerful deep red 'Oscar' have begun showing up on the shelves at supermarkets.

The red-with-purple-flares variety 'Fire Queen' is a knockout, as is the red-and-yellow species tulip *T. schrenkii* (1585). Two other species tulips that force well are the delicate red-and-yellow *T. clusiana* (1607) and the glorious *T. pulchella violacea,* with small, wine-colored cups and black centers.

Tulips are potted in ordinary potting soil with their noses poking up out of the soil. You will notice that the handsome bulb has one side that is slightly flattened. This flat side should face the outside of the pot because the first leaf to emerge is stored on that side of the bulb and thus, that leaf will drape elegantly over the edge of the pot. (As with other bulbs, the tulip also has a pointy top and a flattened bottom; the pointy end goes up and the flat bottom—not side—goes down.)

Tulips require about a sixteen-week cold period with temperatures around 45°F. They rank up there with crocuses on the rodents' favorite-snack list, so if you are plagued with browsing mice, squirrels, or raccoons, your potted tulips must be secured someplace where those critters can't get to them. When the cold period is complete, move your tulips to a bright, cool (55°F) spot, and blooms will appear in about three weeks.

POTTING-UP DAY

Potting-up day is the moment when you actually plant your bulbs in their pots. Potting up is a term that gardeners use to describe working in containers—if you said that you "planted your bulbs," the assumption would be that you put them outside in your garden. "Potting up" is a friendly, old-fashioned term that here signifies your first step in the gentle art of forcing.

If you wisely choose to forgo forcing bulbs for the December holidays, you can safely schedule your potting-up day for a crisp, blue-skied October day when your innate energy for hunting, gathering, and putting up for winter is buzzing. A warm, sunny spot outside on a picnic table or inside in the kitchen will make this pleasantly messy task even more fun. Although some books recommend embarking on a series of potting-up days, this isn't really necessary. One day during the first couple of weeks in October will result in waves of flowers in February and March.

Gearing Up. Besides bulbs, you'll need the following: pots with drainage holes, labels, several sharpened pencils, gallon-size clear plastic bags, new potting soil, sand, pebbles, a calendar, and water. If you're working indoors, spread lots of newspapers around because soil inevitably goes everywhere as you plant and water.

Plastic pots are an extremely affordable option, and it's perfectly fine to use them. However, a beautifully weathered plastic pot has yet to grace this earth. Although plastic pots don't dry out as fast as terra-cotta pots, most people agree that the ugliness of plastic just isn't worth it. Plastic pots work well aesthetically if slipped, like a liner, inside a prized cachepot.

You don't have to spend a fortune on clay pots. Home improvement centers carry enormous selections of good-looking clay pots, and if you leave them stacked up on the north side of the house, they'll soon achieve the classic weathered look that older pots have. Before using clay pots, soak them in a bucket of water so they don't wick the moisture out of the soil. If they've been used before, add half a cup of bleach to the water bucket to ward off nasty diseases. (Forced bulbs rarely succumb to disease, but consistently bleaching used pots is simply good horticultural hygiene.)

Putting It All Together. It always makes good sense to use new potting soil with any fresh planting, and bulbs are no exception. Some gardeners prefer one commercial mix over others, and if you have no experience at all with potting soil, it might be a good idea to purchase small bags of several different brands and see which kind suits you best. Experiment with small batches so that you don't get stuck with twenty pounds of potting soil you don't like. Just don't buy potting soil with added fertilizer if you're potting up bulbs for forcing—forced bulbs are finished and gone before they ever need fertilizer.

Some soils are bagged absolutely dry and must be moistened, while others come premoistened. The absolutely dry type weighs less, so if you must haul all supplies up four flights of stairs, this is a big bonus. Mix dry soil with water in a big cooking pot before you begin planting, and expect to make a bit of a mess doing this. Premoistened soils are a bit heavier to lug home from the store, but have the advantage of being quicker and less messy to use because you don't have to add water to them before potting up.

Whether you use premoistened soil or not, you should add sand to bulb-potting soil. Sand helps soil to drain better, and bulbs require quick draining action. Sand will also help prevent the annoying crust that sometimes forms on top of potting soil, making water from subsequent waterings roll right off. To add sand to potting soil, mix three measures of soil to one measure of sand, and repeat these proportions until you have enough mixture for a number of pots. (A big wooden spoon makes a great soil mixer.) You'll know when your preparation is about right when you scoop up a handful of soil and squeeze it in your fist. If water gushes out, it's too wet and you must add more soil. If there are still batches of dry particles, add more water. When you open your fist, the sand and soil mixture should crumble apart. If it stays squeezed into a ball, add a bit more sand to make a looser mix.

Before you put this mixture into your chosen container, add a layer of gravel to the bottom of the pot, making sure that one fat pebble sits directly over the drainage hole. This will prevent your custom-blended, quick-draining soil mix from pouring through the hole with each watering.

As you begin putting soil over the gravel layer in the pot, firm it with the back of a big

∾ RIGHT *Crocus vernus 'Remembrance' (originally bred in 1925) is often found forced in plastic pots in discount malls and grocery stores. It can easily be repotted and displayed with style.*

spoon so that the eventual roots from your bulbs have something to grab onto. Don't add soil all

Bulb Primer

PAPERWHITES

The paperwhite is the prom queen of the narcissus clan. And like all the best prom queens, besides being good-looking, paperwhites have the sturdy disposition and easy likability that account for long-term popularity. Many indoor gardeners whose lives are too busy or whose living quarters are too cramped find forcing paperwhites an easy, quick, and undemanding introduction into the joys of flowering bulbs in winter.

Paperwhites belong to the tazetta division of the genus *Narcissus* and are native to the warm Mediterranean parts of the world. This means that they do not require a cold period to flower, and both water forcing (see page 44) and soil forcing can be accomplished in under a month. Paperwhite bulbs are usually available on the market from autumn through winter, and considering their quick cultivation, you could have prom

queens in your house from early November until late spring. The variety 'Ziva' is snowy white and blooms in as little as two weeks, while the pure white 'Jerusalem' and 'Galilee' bloom in about three weeks. 'Bethlehem,' 'Nazareth,' and 'Israel' also bloom in about three weeks, but each of these have different shades of warm yellow in their blossoms.

When your bulbs arrive, don't place them in the refrigerator or in any other cold place. Store the bulbs in brown paper bags at room temperature in a dark spot. If you want to plant in succession and have waves of flowers in full bloom, check on your unplanted bulbs as time passes to make sure that they aren't sprouting too much. Any bulb that has sprouts over two inches long should be planted within a few days.

For growing paperwhites in pots, place three inches of soil in the bottom of a five-inch deep (or more) pot with good drainage. Place the bulbs as closely together as possible, and add more soil until the bulbs are about half covered. Water thoroughly to settle, then add more soil until the bulbs are about three-quarters covered. Water again and firm soil. Any space left between the bulb and the rim of the pot will support the leaves and blossoms when they appear.

POTTING AND COOLING CHART FOR HARDY BULBS

Bulb	Potting depth	Cold, dark period	Cool, light period
CROCUS	1 inch deep	10–12 weeks	2–3 weeks
HYACINTH	tops of bulbs out	12–15 weeks	2–3 weeks
NARCISSUS (HARDY)	1 inch deep	12–15 weeks	2–4 weeks
TULIP	tops of bulbs out	14–16 weeks	2–4 weeks
IRIS	½ inch deep	12–15 weeks	2–3 weeks
SCILLA	1 inch deep	10–12 weeks	2–4 weeks
PUSCHKINIA	1 inch deep	10–12 weeks	2–3 weeks

the way to the top of the pot because you still need to add your bulbs and the soil that will cover them. Also, you'll want to allow extra room at the top to ensure that water can soak into the soil instead of rolling off the edges. For example, if you're getting ready to pot crocuses that need to be planted one inch deep, stop adding soil when you're about two inches from the top of the pot. Add the crocus corms, put one inch of soil on top of them, and firm everything into place, making sure the pot rim is higher than the soil level.

Place only one type of bulb in each pot. Although it's pleasant to envision a pot with a mixture of crocuses and small daffodils, the reality is that the crocuses will sprout up first, flower, and be finished before the daffodils get going. It's better to stick to one type of bulb per pot and then, if some things happen to bloom at the same time, display the pots together.

Place the bulbs with their pointy ends up, and for best effect, arrange them as close together as possible without having them actually touch. Ignore any spacing recommendations that might come on packages of hardy bulbs because these refer to outdoor plantings, which multiply over the years. Forcing in pots is a one-season affair. Once the bulbs are snuggled in firmly, cover with soil to the recommended depth and water thoroughly.

The next important stage in potting up is marking your containers. Before you move on from one lot of bulbs to the next, you must identify what you have planted. Fill out a label (dark pencil is best for wooden labels) and stick it into the pot next to the rim. There's nothing worse than trying to remember which bulbs are in what container once you have three different groups of pots sitting in front of you.

Some people also use the label to note the potting date and the day for removing the pot from its cold spot, but this results in a very crowded label. It's usually better to put names on labels and dates on calendars. Put a big circle around potting-up day, consult the cooling chart on the previous page, count the different weeks as recommended, and mark the approximate

⤳ LEFT *Small bulbs like crocuses look best when placed in pots appropriate to their size.* ⤳ RIGHT *Sweetly scented* Crocus chrysanthus *'Snowbunting' (originally bred in 1914) was a favorite of famous American garden writer Elizabeth Lawrence.*

dates when your potted bulbs should progress from one stage to the next.

COURAGEOUS CHILLING METHODS

After potting, the first true stage of forcing bulbs requires a bit of ingenuity. Because hardy bulbs come from temperate climates and require a cold period before blooming, your responsibility is to provide their necessary winter. All kinds of places will fulfill this prerequisite—all you have to do is find one that works best for you.

An old-fashioned rule of thumb regarding chilling is that hardy bulbs need three different stages of temperatures: an extended period around 40°F to develop roots; a shorter period at 50°F to develop foliage and stems; and then temperatures around 60°F to make the best flowers. (Modern books are more precise, prescribing 45° to 48°F for four to eight weeks for root development, 38° to 42°F for nine more weeks for shoot development, and then indoor temperatures of 55° to 60°F for flowering. If these time frames seem confusing, just keep in mind that bulbs stored in unheated places will often automatically experience these temperatures as autumn progresses into winter). Commercial growers have to be very precise with temperatures because they have to deliver goods on time, but the home grower can relax a bit and use a gardener's powers of observation as the best forcing guide.

The Right Spot. The real trick to forcing bulbs is finding places where ideal temperatures can be maintained. Buy a couple of inexpensive thermometers and leave them on the cold side of your unheated garage, on the north side of the attic, underneath the porch stairs, in the potting shed, or in a cold basement. You might be surprised how cold these places stay in late October—especially if you can keep

Bulb Primer

NARCISSUS

The genus *Narcissus* includes many bulbs that are very popular for winter flowering. Some varieties are hardy and require a cold period to flower, but others—especially the paperwhites—are not hardy and have different cultural requirements. See "Paperwhites" on page 38).

As with hyacinths and crocuses, some narcissus varieties can easily be found potted, forced, and ready to bloom in grocery stores and discount centers. These inexpensive little treats are usually the varieties 'Tête à Tête,' 'Ice Follies,' and 'Jack Snipe.'

In order of their cold requirements, 'Rip van Winkle' (1885; also listed as *Narcissus pumilis plenis*) needs a "hard" cold (around 40°F) and responds by shooting up a fluffy blossom that looks like a tow-headed baby after a shampoo. 'Petit Four' is double-flowered, with white petals and an apricot cup, and 'Baby Moon' has thin, grasslike leaves and many small, fragrant flowers.

Those that need a period of moderate cold (temperatures that hover around 45° to 50°F) include 'Orange Queen' (1908), with small daffodil-shaped

golden flowers that bloom very early. The fragrant 'Laurens Koster' (1906) produces clusters of flowers, while *Narcissus* 'Pencrebar' (dating back to 1611) has miniature double flowers.

Three more tender narcissus that add variety to your collection and are forced exactly like paperwhites are 'Avalanche' (also known as 'Seventeen Sisters,' and perhaps dating to the 1700s), the parlor-gardening Victorians' favorite forcer Chinese Sacred Lily (1880s), and 'Romanus, Double Roman' (1576, slightly more difficult to force but worth the trouble).

Plant narcissus bulbs in mid October in regular potting soil, with the tops of the bulbs showing above the soil. After watering well, chill according to whether your variety needs "hard" cold or moderate cold as described above. (For tender narcissus, see page 38.) Hardy narcissus need a cold period of up to fifteen weeks, and after that, two to four weeks in a cool (55°F), light spot. Flower buds will appear in two or three weeks.

Bulb Primer

Water Forcing

Forcing bulbs in water is an acceptable form of horticultural hedonism. But don't try this trick on expensive, rare bulbs because although water forcing produces gloriously quick results, the bulbs are totally spent at the end of the process.

Hyacinths and crocuses are traditional bulbs for water forcing. Store your autumn-delivered bulbs in brown paper bags at temperatures around 45°F. (Again, remember that you have to choose between bulbs and fruit in your refrigerator.) After New Year's, place several bulbs in bowls of pebbles or single bulbs on top of forcing jars. If you're using the pebble method, fill the bowl with several inches of pebbles, place bulbs on top of them, and then fill in around the bulbs with more pebbles. If you're using traditional forcing vases, standard bud vases, or even slanted-side vases, sit each bulb securely, allowing at least several inches of space under its bottom for emerging roots.

Fill the bowl or vase with water until it almost touches the bottom of the bulb,

and place the whole rig in a cool, dark place for rooting. There are those who recommend putting charcoal in the rooting water or periodically changing the water to "keep it sweet" and prevent the growth of algae. But experience has shown that skipping both these procedures produces no harmful effects whatsoever.

Place your bulbs and their water containers inside brown paper grocery bags in a cool (50° to 55°F) place. Keep tabs on them to make sure that water levels remain steady. If no roots appear, add a little more water; if mold appears, keep the water level a tad lower. Roots should sprout in about two weeks, and top shoots will appear shortly thereafter. When crocus top shoots are one inch tall and hyacinth shoots two inches, place water-forced bulbs in a cool, light position where you can admire their noodle-like roots and the impossibly big leaves and buds. The whole show takes about one month from bulb to blossom.

Water forcing tender narcissus and paperwhites is easy, too. These bulbs don't require a cold period—just place them on pebbles or forcing vases as described above, and put them in a cool (55°F) room inside a brown paper grocery bag. Roots will quickly appear, followed by a top shoot. When they're two inches tall, bring them into a light room but keep them away from direct sun. If the plant starts to get top-heavy, prop it up with twigs or a tiny tepee made of sticks, or bend a section of the small, decorative wire fence used for garden edging to fit the pot.

the sun out with layers of newspaper or card-board. Cold frames also make excellent chilling spots, as long as deep snows that come later don't freeze them shut. Spare refrigerators are ideal but never store bulbs and fruit in the same place. Ripening fruit produces ethylene gas, which causes bulbs to make deformed flowers.

Once you've decided on the perfect cold spot, move all your potted bulbs there. It's help-ful to leave a thermometer at the spot, too, so you can monitor how chilling progresses. Some people place each pot in a clear one-gallon plas-tic bag, sealed to help with moisture retention. This is fine as long as you periodically check for mold. If you're afraid of temperatures dropping very low and freezing your containers solid (not good), pack the pots into cardboard boxes filled with plastic peanuts, or use an old styrofoam ice chest as an insulated box. Don't stack your pots on top of each other because some bulbs send up sprouts that will be damaged by the weight of

other pots. It's important to keep everything accessible because you'll have to water during this chilling period.

If you've planted crocuses, tulips, or frit-illaries, it's a fairly good bet that mice will raid your hoard because they find these bulbs

∾ ABOVE *This blue-and-white indoor garden features antique vases, handmade tiles, forced white tulips and hyacinths, and the sprouting buds of amaryllis 'Yellow Pioneer.'*

scrumptious. You can try sprinkling red pepper or using a highly scented room deodorizer to ward them off, but the best bet is to put pots with those bulbs in an old metal footlocker, or in one of the giant plastic storage bins found at big discount stores.

The Waiting Game. During the next two months, you must remember to water regularly. It's easy to forget, so mark reminders on your calendar because this is when the all-important roots are growing. Ninety percent of all forcing failures are due to lack of good roots.

Water until a few drops drain from the bottom of the pot, and water as often as necessary to keep the soil feeling slightly moist to the touch. Take care that the soil doesn't ever get soggy, however, because this will cause the bulbs

☙ LEFT *Indoor flowers need not be extravagant. These lovely forced tulips were purchased from the grocery store for under $2—and repotted into small blue pots that also cost less than $2.*

to rot. A general rule of thumb is to water once a week, but always check for dryness by the middle of each week.

If you notice the tops of the bulbs growing at this stage, try to lower the temperature a little to slow this action down. Open the garage door to the north wind, shield pots from daytime sun, or turn the heat a little lower, but don't worry too much about a few days of balmy weather. If you potted up when the weather was turning cold, nature will take care of this part of the chilling requirements.

If you potted up during the first weeks of October, you should begin seeing some rooted results right after New Year's Day. To check on this, turn one of your smallest pots sideways in your hand and gently tap the soil a little way out of the pot. You should see white roots at least two inches long. Carefully resettle the bulb and soil back into the pot, water, and be satisfied that everything is on track. After root formation, watch for pale emerging shoots as a signal to begin the next forcing stage.

Keep It Cool. After your bulbs have satisfied their cold rooting requirements and produced shoots one to two inches tall, it's time to put them in a cool (around 50°F), light location inside the house. A guest room or an empty-nest room where you can close the door and turn down the heat is particularly handy for this. Strong direct sunlight is a killer at this stage of the game, so a northern exposure is terrific. Buy inexpensive disposable aluminum foil cake pans—like those used for bake sales—to protect floors and windowsills. Then bring in some of the earliest bloomers like crocuses and hyacinths, keep them watered, and watch carefully. As those little shoots begin to grow and turn green, magic is getting ready to happen. Depending on the bulb, you'll have flowers in anywhere from two to three weeks. Not every bulb will bloom, but even a first-timer can expect to have at least a fifty percent success rate for flowering.

PRESENTATION
IS EVERYTHING

Forcing hardy bulbs is a horticultural tour de force. It is truly disappointing, therefore, when someone spends several months of time and effort to beautifully accomplish the job, but doesn't expend one minute on showing off those bulbs properly. If you have a child who is a violin prodigy, surely you wouldn't send her off for her Carnegie Hall debut in her pajamas. Likewise, don't expect any swooning over your gorgeous 'Rip Van Winkle' daffodils forced indoors if they're in unattractive plastic pots with mud dripped over the side. Primping plants and fussing over their appearance is a big part of the satisfaction of growing things. Indulge yourself in this creative part of indoor gardening so your

 LEFT *This indoor garden features a hand-forged* tutuer *with climbing ivy, a large pot of tender phormiums, forced irises, narcissus, ranunculus, snowdrops, and a few primroses.*

plants will look happy and tidy, and your house will look even better.

Putting Them in Place. The first caveat for forced bulbs is that they do not tolerate heat at all. One night on the mantel with a fire roaring in the grate and those 'Fire Queen' tulips are goners. But if you put the pot in a cool, north-facing window (not just above the radiator, please), 'Fire Queen' will light up your breakfasts for at least a week.

For any forced bulb, once the leaves have greened and the buds are set during the second stage of forcing, providing light is no longer necessary. This means that you can make a row of crocus pots across a sideboard, perch a hyacinth on a bookshelf, or wake up to the scent of tiny irises on your bedside table. Think of these little charmers as a movable feast, and because all flowers are ephemeral, enjoy them as much as possible while they're fresh.

Although forced bulbs look sweet lined

up along a windowsill, especially when snow is piled high outdoors, avoid putting them in a window where the sun beats down—this will end your show all too soon. As long as you protect fine furniture from scratches and water damage (always use a saucer under pots when displaying indoors), you can place your gorgeous bulbs almost anyplace where temperatures stay cool. For example, if you want to put a pot of crocuses next to your reading chair, remember that when you turn on the light, the heat produced from close exposure to the light bulb will likely cause your crocuses to sulk.

Make the Most of It. You can enjoy other people's forced bulbs, too. Although it may seem unlikely, bulbs in flower actually take to transplantation very well. So if you're making a bulk grocery buy at the local discount mart and suddenly notice racks and racks of forced tulips, crocuses, and narcissus, grab a few pots. These inexpensive bijoux will undoubtedly be in hideous plastic pots wrapped in garish foil. Never mind, just water the pots well and tap the bottom with a firm but gentle action until the entire root ball comes out into your hand. Repot into nice containers, or you may separate the bulbs into several different pots. Four pots of tiny 'Tête à Tête' daffodils can be gathered into a gossipy bunch in an old cast-iron planter, or a half-dozen white tulips divided into six small blue pots. Usually, commercially produced bulbs are in a very lightweight potting medium and have been grown at such optimum conditions that transplanting store-bought forced bulbs causes no setbacks whatsoever.

Home-forced bulbs can be transplanted, too. If your pot of 'Generaal de Wet' tulips has three great-looking flowers and two deformed

∽ RIGHT *A cool north window is a perfect spot for displaying forced* Tulipa *'Monte Carlo' and inky purple* Iris histrioides *'George' with a few twigs, also ready for forcing.*

ones that a naughty mouse chewed on, take a dinner fork and ease the good ones out (roots intact) into a smaller pot. Fill in with soil as necessary, water well, and no one will know the difference. Generally, home-forced bulbs are a little trickier to move around, but if you take care to water well afterward, no harm should result. If a stem does break, just put the remains in your best bud vase and it will still open up and flower.

If you've used plastic pots inside your cachepots, make sure that the plastic edges don't show up like the floral equivalents of a panty line. Once each plastic pot is securely placed, add a scattering of fresh soil and a handful of pine needles or some pretty pebbles to keep the unattractive edges hidden.

Mixing and Matching. Deciding what bulbs to put in what container can cause a bottleneck on potting-up day. The best advice is not to agonize too much because this process gets simpler with experience. The first year you force bulbs is similar to the first time you were allowed to purchase your own clothes. Too many choices can be overwhelming, so the best thing to do is assemble an assortment of suitable containers in a variety of shapes and sizes. When you begin, stick to basic shapes and classic neutral colors. But if you happen to see a great container lurking in a shop, buy it and bring it home. You won't regret this sort of impulse purchase when you later discover that the shiny red glaze looks terrific with dark purple tulips.

There's no iron-clad rule about matching bulbs and pots except that small bulbs do tend to look lost in great big pots. Since their leaves and flowers tend to be less voluminous, you end up with lots of small spots of color in a mass of potting soil. Even with bigger bulbs, you probably won't need any pots that are deeper than six inches, or more than six inches across the top. Long-term cultivation needs are not a consideration when forcing bulbs, so one tiny crocin in a tiny pot can work just fine for one short season.

Terra-cotta pots and plants are perfect together, and glazed pots also show off plants beautifully. A green pot emphasizes the green throat of *Iris histrioides* 'George,' and yellow *I. danfordiae* positively shines from the confines of a matte black pot. Many tulips have leaves with a slightly glaucous or bluish green hue and look especially wonderful paired with pots glazed a grayish blue. It's sometimes difficult to guess good pot and plant matches in advance, but as your bulbs come into bloom this winter, observe that those yellow 'Monte Carlo' tulips would look terrific in that pale orange square pot. It's no more difficult than matching curtain fabric to wall color, but this simple feat can transform a humble Cinderella of a daffodil into a very special 'Orange Queen.'

∾ RIGHT *A slender twig prevents* Hyacinthus *'Splendid Cornelia' from swan-diving out of its vase.*

Many potting soil mixtures contain quantities of small white styrofoam pieces to make the soil weigh less. After months of watering, these white bits make their way to the surface and sit there like polka dots, distracting from your beautiful crocuses or tulips. If the polka dots bug you, simply pick them out or sprinkle a layer of pure black potting soil (keep a bag on hand) on top of the styrofoam just as your bulbs are ready to do their thing. This may seem beyond reasonable primping, but it takes little time and effort and makes an enormous improvement in a plant's overall appearance.

Putting on a Show. Almost everyone has been to a flower show at some point, but these horticultural extravaganzas are more about showmanship than creating a welcoming, warm atmosphere with plants. Some people like to mass all their pots in one place, shifting things in and out of the spotlight as they peak. Others prefer to scatter pots here and there. Besides remembering to avoid hot spots, the only rule of thumb concerning bulb displays is that highly scented bulbs such as narcissus and hyacinths

✿ LEFT *Pale blue puschkinias make great additions to a forced bulb display.*

can be terrific to perfume the entryway, but might prove overwhelming in a dining room. Some people don't mind the mixture of sweet scents and roast beef, but many do.

It's great fun to figure out how to display groups of bulbs. A slate-topped table is a gorgeous way to show off your efforts. The stone looks perfectly harmonious with terra-cotta or glazed containers, and pots can sit directly on the slate and be watered without damaging the surface. For nighttime drama, scatter a few candles and perhaps add a gorgeous bowl filled to the brim with water, and your slate table will become a showstopper.

Trays can also protect tabletops from moist pots of bulbs. Even an old black metal tray that's seen better days takes on a new elegance when dusted, polished, and lined with pots of yellow daffodils. Likewise, the silver tray that hasn't seen the light of day since your tennis victory during the Labor Day Tournament of 1972 will shine once again under a pot of white tulips. Old or new tiles look great with plants, and a tile-topped tray or mosaic-tile table provides another pretty way to display plants.

Once the blooming period is past, toss bulbs on the compost heap. There's little point in spending several years trying to revitalize forced hardy bulbs when you should really put your energy into thinking about what you'd like to try next. It's a good idea to mark what bloomed when on your forcing calendar, and to make notes about things you might want to try for next winter. Circle the first of August as a good time to look at all of next season's bulb catalogs. Make a reminder to place your orders before Labor Day, and remember to reserve a potting-up day for sometime during the first weeks of October. All of a sudden, you'll realize that there's a fascinating little cycle of gardening happening right inside your house.

CHAPTER TWO tender bulbs: the unforced

TRY A LITTLE TENDERNESS

JUST AS THE FASHION FOR STRIPED CANNAS and enormous elephant's ears brought color and excitement to our outdoor gardens, a revived interest in tender bulbs has definitely put pizzazz back into the modern indoor garden. Before you discount the idea of growing bold red amaryllis or a pot of pink oxalis, consider the fact that nothing can drive you into a boring gardening rut like growing the same plants year after year. For a change of pace, cultivate a few tender bulbs and watch as these exotics add creative spice to your indoor scene.

Tenders Through Time. Some tender bulbs are true tropicals, hailing from areas of South America and Asia located between the latitudes of Capricorn and Cancer. Many of the

LEFT *Tender bulbs like orange clivia, amaryllis, and tall new leaves of elephant's ears (Colocasia esculenta) bring a festive atmosphere to midwinter.*

most popular tender bulbs, however, originate from Cape Province of South Africa. For its size, this part of the Southern Hemisphere is one of the planet's richest places for bulbs. During the time when trading ships sailed around the Cape

of Good Hope, the area became the seagoing version of the biggest and richest truck stop in the world.

Beginning in the 1600s, sailors, traders, and merchants stopped off in the port at Table Bay to restock provisions. On the way back, these wayfarers also collected easily transportable bulbs as souvenirs or as items to sell when they returned home. Native South African plants quickly became commonplace potted up inside European houses, far from the wilds of Cape Town.

Much later, when the Victorians made parlor gardening an edifying art, these straightlaced indoor gardeners first experimented with forcing hardy bulbs, and then fell for tenders. They dabbled in oxalis, but by the mid 1800s calla lilies became the rage.

∾ LEFT *Tender cyclamens are especially popular with indoor gardeners who like to keep their houses on the cool side.*

Tender bulbs like oxalis, cyclamens, and freesias provided flowers that remain popular to this day, but it's shocking to look at a catalog from the late nineteenth century and count all the tender bulbs that have disappeared from popular horticulture. While heirloom tomatoes have been saved by enthusiasts who collect and pass along seeds, it might be too late for many once-popular tender bulbs such as *Bessera, Blandfordia, Bloomeria, Bobartia, Bomaria,* and *Boussingaultia.* After you grow a few of the more well-known bulbs and get the hang of the genre, consider moving on to the cultivation of lesser-known types. And if you make a point of showing off your tender bulbs during their luscious wintertime bloom, your friends might soon join in the movement to rescue endangered bulbs.

∽ RIGHT Amaryllis *'Germa' (properly known as* Hippeastrum *'Germa') has smaller bulbs than most members of this genus. The pale yellow-green flowers open in succession for many weeks.*

SUMMER COMES TO THE SOUTHERN HEMISPHERE

Tender bulbs are perfect for people with parsimonious tendencies. Clusters of orange clivias or the rolled vellum of calla lilies create big drama indoors, but these beauties are not fated to tragic

endings. Unlike hardy bulbs, which are tossed on the compost heap after their sped-up, out-of-season performances, tender bulbs are not thrown out after they flower.

Tender bulbs are not really *forced* into bloom. Those that come from the Southern Hemisphere bloom naturally during our winter because the months of January, February, and March mark their homeland's most salubrious growing season. Bulbs from tropical regions simply respond to their natural growth timetable when you supply the warmth and moisture abundant in their native lands.

With no forced cold periods or chilling times to contend with, tender bulbs lead a much more laid-back lifestyle than their hardy cousins. They naturally bloom in (our) winter and rest up in dormancy during (our) summer. After

∾ LEFT *This arrangement of potted amaryllis includes (from left to right) 'Germa,' 'Appleblossom,' 'Green Goddess,' 'Jewel,' and (lower right) 'Red Lion.' The group stayed in bloom for a month.*

their rest, they will begin to grow and bloom again the following autumn and winter. Their needs during dormancy vary from tender to tender, but are generally quite minimal, so it's not difficult to keep tender bulbs for many years.

MAKING IT MOIST

With the exception of amaryllis, tender bulbs in this section are not suitable for water forcing. One of the major charms of tender bulbs is that they stick around for season after season, whereas water forcing is a one-way road to brief glory and then a swift demise. Water, however, is an extremely important component in the life of a tender bulb—many of them require a healthy amount of moisture. If your house is dry as a desert during the heating months, your must figure a way to up the ante on humidity.

Adding moisture to your indoor environment can be done with relative ease. In many

cases, filling pretty bowls to the brim with water and placing them in sunny windows, near heating ducts, and on top of radiators will do the job. (You'll probably be astonished to discover that these will need topping-up almost every day.) You can also add humidity by leaving the bathroom door open during long, steamy showers. Periodic spritzing with a hand mister, and even draping freshly washed sweaters around the house will add a good amount of moisture to the air. Not only will your tender bulbs benefit from the added water, but so will your skin.

WHEN DARKNESS FALLS

Tender bulbs have distinct dormant periods. In their backward way, they rest and rejuvenate beginning in (our) summer. Many will stop growing and die back completely to the bulbs,

∾ LEFT *The emerging green shoots on these amaryllis bulbs mean that they should be planted immediately.*

and require no care whatsoever all summer. This, of course, makes them very appealing to people who find themselves with tons of other things to do during the summer months. This also means that you must remember to order your tender bulbs during summer because mail-order catalogs ship them during their dormant period. Using the same calendar that was employed for your hardy bulbs projects, mark midsummer as the time for brushing off your catalogs and ordering your tenders.

Tender bulbs usually arrive on the doorstep in the warm part of early autumn. As confirmed individualists, each one will come with its own instructions for potting and growing. For example, the tiny black corms of the wondrous melasphaerula are planted one inch deep; the bulb that produces the vivacious

veltheimia protrudes halfway out of the soil; and the weirdly wonderful bowiea perches right on top of its pot like a fat old pasha relaxing at a picnic.

It's a good idea to keep the instructions that the bulb companies send. If you haven't

≈ RIGHT *Oxalis bulbs sprout very quickly and need direct sunlight to prevent the foliage and flowers from getting too lanky.*

Bulb Primer

AMARYLLIS

(*Hippeastrum*)

Number one among tender bulbs is the big, bold, bawdy amaryllis. Some gardeners swear by their secateurs that they would never bother growing an enormous, garish red amaryllis, and they just can't imagine enjoying a candy-pink one, either. This is all a matter of mind-set.

First of all, the cliché of huge amaryllis blooming among pine branches and fake snow during the December holidays has become, like a frantic hostess, a little too exhausted to be fun. Amaryllis look more appropriate around February or March, when the sunlight is growing strong and the desire for a fiesta makes everyone a little loose. Think of the giant amaryllis 'Red Lion' and the divine pink 'Apple Blossom' as harbingers of a big party, and soon you'll have rearranged all previous arguments against amaryllis.

Most bulbs called amaryllis belong to the genus *Hippeastrum,* but this name is not used widely by home gardeners. Some catalogs list them as *Amaryllis* and send bulbs with pot tags printed *Hippeastrum.* Call them what you like, but do try several different types this winter.

Not all amaryllis are red or pink. 'Rilona' is pale salmon, 'Germa' is greenish yellow, 'Jewel'—with a lilylike, semi-double white flower—has a delicate fragrance. All these have stalks about two and a half to three feet tall, topped with as many as four flowers per stalk. And, as some bulbs throw up three stalks, they may produce a dozen large flowers from one bulb.

GROWING. It is extremely easy to grow amaryllis, and to keep them year after year. The bulbs arrive in autumn and should be stored in paper bags in a cool (around 55°F), dark place until after the new year begins. Amaryllis are potted up in clay pots that are only one inch larger in diameter than the bulb. Firm the soil well, water sparingly once, and then place in a warm (60°F) position out of direct sunlight. Don't water them again until the flower bud and stalk appear, usually in two weeks to a month. Once growth begins, the pot should be watered regularly through blooming and the ripening of foliage. As with other bulbs, water as often as necessary to keep the soil slightly moist to the touch. Water until a few drops drain from the hole in the bottom of the pot. Because an amaryllis produces so much plant in such a small pot, you may find that it needs watering almost every day.

DORMANCY. It's simple to have your amaryllis make return performances each year. The flowers will be gorgeous for about three weeks. After they fade, cut off the stalks and watch the foliage emerge. Keep the plants watered and fertilized through the rest of the cold weather season, and when outside temperatures are consistently above 55°F at night, slowly introduce your amaryllis to the outside world. Keep the pots in a warm, semi-shaded position, and in Sep-

tember begin witholding water to encourage dormancy. Amaryllis can be stubborn about entering dormancy—be firm and don't give them any more water or you probably won't get flowers again next winter. Once foliage has died back, and before frost comes, store potted bulbs (totally dry) in the same cool, dark place where you first kept them.

WATER FORCING. In this chapter, amaryllis is the exception to the rule about not forcing tender bulbs in water. Simply wedge the bulb into the top of a large vase of water and place it in a light, warm place. Flowers will appear in one month. After the show, discard the entire plant on the compost pile.

The water-forced amaryllis flowers are just as long lasting as those forced in soil, but the bulbs cannot be saved for the next year. Water forcing totally deflates these large bulbs—almost like a slow leak eventually flattens a beach ball. For this reason, don't water force rare, expensive bulbs—just ones that you don't mind throwing away after the show.

Amaryllis are notoriously top-heavy and work best when forced inside a deep vase filled with gravel for ballast. Place the bulb midway down the vase so the tall sides help support the stems and foliage as they grow.

established some sort of garden journal for filing and organizing information, you're going to be sorry next September when you can't remember how to rev up these bulbs again. Even a shoebox stuffed with papers can yield just the right bit of information when you really need it.

BREAKING DORMANCY

Most tender bulbs are potted as soon as they arrive at your house. In general, they like good potting medium mixed with sand (see page 36) to provide excellent drainage. It is important to use the pot size recommended by the supplier because some tender bulbs will *not* bloom unless crowded. Also, because many tender bulbs (like amaryllis and veltheimias) are top-heavy, use a heavy clay pot to give them that much more ballast.

Once your tender bulb is planted according to instructions, it is usually watered once *very sparingly* to settle the soil. Dormant bulbs hate to sleep in a damp bed and are prone to rotting if wet. Pat the soil down well, say some magic planting words, and place the pot in a warm spot away from direct sun. Then leave that bulb alone—totally alone. Treat your tender bulb as you would a two-year-old child who is getting ready to wake up after a nap—don't rush the issue. Once the first shoots appear you can begin watering and pampering, but before that signal, it's strictly hands-off.

From the emergence of tiny sprouts, to the formation of foliage, and all during the excitement of flowers, tender bulbs are show-stoppers. The appearance of amaryllis stalks can sometimes astonish the fainthearted, while the crispy rosette that veltheimia throws looks almost edible. As little spears of melasphaerula

∽ RIGHT *These mystery clivias and their pots were purchased from a gardener at a church fair. They are similar to* Clivia miniata, *but their leaves and flowers are arranged more loosely.*

CLIVIA

The orange-flowering evergreen clivia is from South Africa. It is actually easier to grow than amaryllis, and was quite popular from the mid 1800s right through the 1950s. Clivias have always had their loyal fans, however, and one of these caused a stir in the news not long ago because he was selling bulbs from his special rare yellow clivia for $75 apiece. This caused outcries about extravagance, but if you really want a yellow clivia, they are now available.

Clivias are perfect bloomers for people with very little sun. In fact, if the dark green strappy leaves of this plant turn brown at the tips, it's a sign to move the plant further into the shade without delay. There's nothing like a large group of clivias to light up a shadowy corner, and once you've found their perfect spot, you never have to move them again. In fact, for four months of the year you don't even have to water them—and the

leaves still look as glossy and healthy as ever. Clivias are the perfect tender bulbs for those who expect big rewards from very little effort.

GROWING. Clivias are usually purchased already potted (and sometimes already in bloom) from your nearest commercial greenhouse. They despise being repotted and usually are happy crowded into the same container for a decade or more. When repotted they may sulk, so most professional growers wait several seasons after dividing before selling them so customers will be satisfied with the flowers.

And the flowers are certainly satisfying. Most well-established *Clivia miniata* make large umbels of ten to twenty flowers, with individual blossoms reaching almost two inches in diameter. The species *C. nobilis* is slightly smaller, but also produces great umbels of flowers. Keep both varieties watered regularly, making an effort to water around—not on—the fleshy, thickened root bulb, and also avoiding wetting the leaves. Clivias prefer things to stay on the dryish side, so let the top half-inch of soil get dry before watering. At that time, add enough water for a few drops to appear on the saucer underneath the pot.

DORMANCY. As flowers fade, deadhead regularly and more clusters will probably appear. This sherbet-colored show lasts almost the entire month of March, and then you're left with those wonderfully glossy leaves. Keep watering all through summer and autumn until the first day of November. On that day, stop watering and don't begin again until the first day of March. This is how clivia is led into dormancy, but no one will ever suspect that those pretty plants in the corner are in a state of suspended animation.

shoot upward like a tiny lawn on steroids, and your bowiea produces snakes of vines like bright green Play-Doh pasta, you'll soon realize that the great thing about growing tender bulbs is that the whole show happens right before your eyes.

BACK TO SLEEP

Most of the tender bulbs included here have their heyday of flowering during February and March. After the flowers fade, you'll need to "ripen" the foliage (this builds up the bulbs for flowering next year) and then encourage dormancy. Tender bulbs usually let you know when it's time to go back to sleep because they begin to get ragged looking. The lush, grasslike foliage of melasphaerula turns brown, the colorful leaves of oxalis look shopworn, and the vining bowiea becomes distinctly limp. This is the time to slowly let the soil dry up and to encourage the plant to go into full rest.

Most tenders go back to sleep easily, but amaryllis often must be coaxed into resting, and clivia has an eerie evergreen dormancy. But in general, this is the time when you stop watering, remove the pots from direct sunlight, and let all action cease. When the foliage completely withers, cut it off at soil level and follow individual instructions for best dormancy locations. Some bulbs prefer being unpotted and stored in bags until next autumn, while others will sulk if they are not left alone in the same pot for decades.

Tender bulbs require a little individual attention, but the rewards of growing them are thrilling. They are surprisingly easy to keep from year to year, and their wintertime appearance reminds us that there is a big world outside our snug homes. As you place your orders, you'll discover the vast network of savvy afficionados who supply these more unusual bulbs, and their enthusiasm will likely carry over to you. Begin this winter with several of the tried-and-true

tenders that follow. Soon you'll find that tender bulbs aren't tough, and that a whole new hemisphere of bulbs awaits its welcome into your abode. Growing something new is the best way to overcome any horticultural doldrums and introduce new plants, new colors, and new fragrances into your environs. At the very least, you'll never regret trying.

HOW TO BUY
TENDER BULBS

Although the usual red and pink types of amaryllis are widely available from standard bulb catalogs, most other tender bulbs are sold through specialty catalogs (an annotated list is included in the Resource Guide on page 151). Tender bulbs are shipped during their summer

∾ LEFT *The old-fashioned tender bulb* Scilla peruviana *is an excellent choice for a cool house. This plant is dormant from August until November.*

dormant period, so you must request catalogs in early spring and order by summer for fall shipping. Tenders cannot be shipped once the weather gets cold because they will die if exposed to prolonged cold, even when boxed up in their dormant state.

You can also purchase tender bulbs in full leaf (and sometimes in flower) from any old-fashioned greenhouse that devotes space to this unusual sort of plant. (Nowadays, many modern greenhouses have gone into mass growings of rather ordinary things.) Tender bulbs purchased during their active growth period have been planted and grown on, and are usually available in midwinter just as they are setting buds. Purchasing bulbs from a good greenhouse also allows you access to the experts who grow the plants, and their advice is invaluable.

When you purchase tender bulbs already in growth, be careful to keep the plants warm all the way home. One sustained blast of

Bulb Primer

BOWIEA

If you're looking for something a little unusual, bowiea is a perfect candidate. In fact, the biggest know-it-all in your garden club will be stumped by this astonishing addition to your obviously superior exotic plant collection. Just don't let on that bowiea is so easy to grow that it actually belongs to your ten-year-old son—and that he loves it because it's downright weird. Bowiea's fat bright green bulbs perch right on top of the soil, and from a small opening on top, they send up long, grasping vines that look like alien tentacles.

GROWING. Bowiea bulbs are available during their May-to-October dormancy period. The large green bulbs are fragile and will scar if scratched, so handle them carefully. Unlike other bulbs, scratches matter here because bowiea bulbs sit right on top of the soil in the

pot, and their plump, shiny greenness is part of their charm. Just nestle the bulb into a pot filled with sandy potting mix, moisten slightly, and wait until sprouts appear.

During this waiting period, keep yourself occupied by making a trellis or tepee out of sticks about four feet tall. Believe it or not, what emerges from that squat, shiny bulb is going to climb at least that tall. In subsequent years, it may take over an entire warm, sunny window. Well-established bowieas have been known to climb up to fifteen feet.

Once sprouting starts, keep bowieas well watered. The fleshy stems will climb upward on their own, so there's no need to twist or tie them. The stems will branch repeatedly, and when mature will produce soft little clouds of starry greenish flowers.

By May the vines will start to wither and you can put the whole thing away until next October. Stop watering at this point and when the vines have completely dried up, cut them off the bulb. Leave the bulbs right in their soil and pot, but since bowiea bulbs sit high, invert another pot on top as a lid to keep everything in the dark. This will help keep the bulbs dormant until next autumn. Store the entire business in a warm, dry spot such as a warm closet or under the back stairs.

wind at 30°F will cause any greenhouse plant to keel over in an unattractive, frostbitten mess. And unlike forced hardy bulbs, which are easy to repot at any time, tender bulbs should not be moved from their pots while they are in active growth. They may refuse to flower. The only safe time to repot tender bulbs is during their dormant period.

Another place to hunt around for dormant tender bulbs is at ordinary plant centers. Increasingly, these stores feature large display areas with cardboard bins full of surprisingly good bulb selections. The only caveats here are the lack of experts on hand and the fact that there are no guarantees. As a beginner, it's better to take the safer route with speciality catalogs and greenhouses. Once you've gained several years' experience, then take a few chances.

RIGHT Tender clivias need a dormant period of several months, during which time all water is withheld. The leaves that remain are evergreen and fresh, but clivias will refuse to flower next winter without a dry spell.

Bulb Primer

MELASPHAERULA

There has only ever been one melasphaerula species, and it has almost disappeared from indoor cultivation. This little South African native was introduced into Europe in 1786. The Victorians called it fairy bells, and the 1886 edition of *The Illustrated Dictionary of Gardening* praised melasphaerula with glowing terms: "very pretty . . . an elegant and graceful habit . . . a profusion of flowers . . . in perfection for a considerable time."

Melasphaerula is absolutely easy to grow. Plant it, leave it in the same pot forever, give it a minimum amount of attention, and watch it produce a maximum amount of wintertime wonder.

∾ LEFT *The last blooms of these clivias decorate a cool window, along with a handmade tripod supporting climbing vines of tender bowiea.*

GROWING. The tiny black corms of melasphaerula are planted in late autumn, and you can pack about twenty-five together in a pot seven inches across and four inches deep. Follow the no-watering rule until you see tips of green. Over the next several months, melasphaerula will make a great show of grassy leaves that eventually reach about fifteen inches tall. These can get floppy, so it's a good idea to make some sort of stick support—a miniature version of the wooden guards put around newly planted trees works quite well to keep the leaves upright and uncreased (see page 77).

Melasphaerula does not require lots of watering or sun, and just when you begin to think that the foliage alone is nice, long wiry stems will begin to twist up through the leaves. Each stem eventually yields up to a dozen small white or pale yellow flowers with deep purple marks on the inside of each petal. The stems and flowers last almost the entire month of March and have the sweetest way of wafting around on breezes made when you walk past the pot. The tiny flowers are too delicate to be seen from a distance, so make sure you place your melasphaerula where its dainty charms can be fully appreciated.

DORMANCY. Melasphaerula behaves like other South African bulbs and declines in late spring. Stop watering and let the leaves totally wither before you cut them off at soil level. For summer storage, use a pot saucer as a lid to keep all water and rain from touching the soil inside the pot, and put this snug little arrangement outside where the pot will bake in the hot sun. Place a brick on top of the lid to make sure the cat doesn't knock it over while chasing moles in the garden beds.

Bulb Primer

OXALIS

Why on earth are the weedy old oxalis found here in the company of all these special bulbs? The reason is that they are not the weedy oxalis that will one day overtake California. The oxalis here are entirely well-behaved, desirable, and have no intentions of going anywhere besides the sunniest windowsill you can provide.

Oxalis are often grown for the foliage alone. The type called 'Iron Cross' makes a rounded mass of deep purple leaves that look like someone cut them out of squares of paper. Other oxalis types are sold around St. Patrick's Day as pots of shamrocks, and most people forget that if they just keep them watered and in the sun, these sweet plants will make lots of delicate flowers in white, pink, or yellow. The old-fashioned candy-stripe oxalis has much skinnier leaves, but when it slowly upwraps its pink-and-white-striped flowers in the morning sun, you'll be so fascinated you might be late to work.

Oxalis bulbs are small, so the plants look best when planted close together in

small pots. Cover them with one inch of soil, water once, and firm the soil with the back of a spoon. Don't water again until sprouts appear. Oxalis thrives in direct light and warmth, so place the pot in the sunniest window you have. As the leaves begin to unfold from the soil, be sure to turn your pot daily or everything will end up smashed against the window. As the leaves begin to fill out, separate flower stems will appear and cheerful flowers will begin to unroll. Because oxalis likes to sit in a warm, sunny spot, evaporation will be rapid and the plants will probably need to be watered almost every day. On dark, rainy days the flowers may not open, but your plant will probably continue to bloom for about six weeks.

Like other tender bulbs, oxalis needs a dormant period after all the excitement of flowering is over. When the foliage begins to dry up, stop watering and allow everything to wither. When the foliage has totally dried, cut it off at the soil line, cover the pot with a saucer as a lid, and place the plant in a warm, dry spot. Leave this absolutely alone until next autumn, when the whole sweet routine begins again.

SUPPORT SYSTEMS

Some tender bulbs, like veltheimias and callas, are sturdy growers that require no outside support. Others, like melasphaerulas and bowieas, get very untidy unless you fashion a small trellis or fence for them to lean or climb on. Many amaryllis also grow tall stalks with such enthusiasm that they also require some help holding up their enormous flowers. Creating an indoor support system may involve nothing more than a few twigs, but once you get the hang of it, you can add individual flair with small stick sculptures.

Melasphaerulas, which have long, grassy leaves, need a support constructed somewhat like a small tower to keep those leaves from sprawling. To form the uprights, poke four straight sticks (about eighteen inches tall) into the soil, equidistant from each other. The uprights should be next to the rim of the pot so that the eventual enclosed area is as large as

∾ ABOVE *Sprays of forced willows are framed by half of a double gothic twig trellis. Made of apple tree prunings supplied by a local arborist, the trellis will support leaning or climbing tenders.*

possible. Next, lash slender twigs horizontally between the uprights with natural garden twine. Two or three sets of horizontal twigs evenly spaced up the upright "posts" will keep the support from being too wobbly. This trellis system doesn't need to support any weight since the foliage is as light as feathers—the trellis simply needs to keep the leaves from falling over. If you like, you can go for a more free-form approach, but just remember to guide the emerging foliage to grow up inside the tiny trellis so that it receives the full benefit of support.

Since bowiea produces a climbing vine, it will enjoy growing on a "jungle gym." You can purchase a wire topiary form and let the bowiea scamper over this, or you can use the pretty metal indoor obelisks that are now widely available. If you want to stay with hand-built structures, constructing a climbing rig for bowiea is very simple. Four bendable sticks about four feet long are necessary. If these are unavailable, pur-chase four slender bamboo stakes of the same length from a plant center. Either way, poke the four sticks into the soil at the rim of tie the pot, and tie the tops together with a piece of string to form a tepee shape. The bendable sticks will bow gracefully while the bamboo will not. There's no need to add horizontal rails to this trellis. Guide the emerging bowiea vine to one of the uprights and it will naturally grab on and climb gracefully to the top, and then begin to drape down like a green fountain. If there are other tall objects or plants nearby, you may find your bowiea wan-dering over for company. This sort of serendipity adds tons of charm to your indoor garden.

Providing support for a top-heavy amaryl-lis practically requires an engineering degree. There is no room for poking heavy stick trellises into the soil because these huge bulbs prefer to be crammed into small pots. Sometimes, how-ever, one strong stick can be wedged in, hidden behind the stem. Using green twine, tie the stick

Bulb Primer

VELTHEIMIA

Veltheimia is another tender bulb that was once wildly popular but faded from view in the 1950s. For those whose taste in decor has swung back to that decade's curvy coffee tables and stiffly shaped sofas, this is the perfect tender bulb. It is more sculptured than soft, yet there's a real retro appeal to its shape and color. Be warned, however, that veltheimia is probably not the first tender bulb you should try because it isn't a guaranteed bloomer every time.

GROWING. The veltheimia offered most often in catalogs has shiny bright green leaves, but there is also one with knockout bluish green leaves. Both are cultivated in the same manner. Pot up with most of the bulb sticking out of the soil. Soon, a crispy rosette of leaves appears and the sculptured growth begins. Veltheimias prefer temperatures on the cool side, and the leaves hate

direct sunlight. If the foliage starts looking unhappy, move the pot away from the window and the heater.

Around February a flower stalk will start to grow and may top three feet before a raceme of densely packed flowers begins to open. The flowers are pink and tubular, and as they mature, the tall stem may take on a purplish blue tint. The flower lasts at least two weeks, giving you plenty of time to position your veltheimia on that curvy coffee table, zip yourself into a cocktail dress, and invite some friends over to celebrate.

DORMANCY. After flowering, treat veltheimias like most other South African bulbs. Ripen the foliage until it begins to turn brown in early summer, and then let it die back into dormancy. Store the potted bulb where it will stay warm and totally dry. Next autumn, retrieve the pot and begin watching your veltheimia for the sprouts that signal its revival.

Even if you're a novice, veltheimia is well worth the added effot. In the realm of successful flower growing, a gardener's desire will often win over inexperience, and veltheimia could be your first horticultural coup.

to the flowering head to lend support. Also, turning your amaryllis away from the light every day will help even out the lopsided tilt.

TENDERS IN THE SUMMER GARDEN

Some tenders, like melasphaerula and oxalis, go into full dormancy before hot weather arrives. With the foliage totally dry and cut off, all you have to do is place the covered pot (usually the saucer serves as a lid) in a warm place and leave it alone until autumn. Covered pots with sleeping bulbs can be placed outside after night temperatures stay above 55°F. They must stay totally dry and toasty warm for their summer camping-out period. But be sure to bring your pots back indoors when the weather gets cold because even dormant tender bulbs hate frost.

Some tender bulbs, like callas and clivias, are still in growth when hot weather comes and will also do very well when moved

⮠ LEFT *These tender cannas, lifted from the autumn garden, can be started indoors in late spring.*
⮠ RIGHT *There are more than 850 species of oxalis.*

Bulb Primer

CALLA LILY

(*Zantedeschia*)

Although Holland suffered a disastrous financial period with tulips and tulipomania in the 1630s, by the middle of the seventeenth century the Dutch were once again dealing in plants. By 1652, the Dutch East India Company controlled the route around South Africa's southern tip as part of their dominant spice trade in the Far East. Part of the strategy was to establish a garden at Table Bay, the harbor area of Cape Town. Fruits and vegetables of all sorts were grown there, which allowed Dutch ships to stock fresh supplies and insured that their sailors and passengers would have a much better chance of surviving the long, perilous journey east.

It was during one of these Cape Town stops that somebody must have noticed the enormously tall calla lilies (reaching up to six feet in the wild) that grow in marshy places all around Table Bay. Although the natives called them pig lilies, the homesick sailors thought they were captivating. Calla rhizomes were collected as souvenirs to be brought home to wives and sweethearts, and by 1687, the stately calla was charming gardeners all over Europe.

The familiar calla lily has a very official proper name. But just as it is unlikely that the home gardener will start calling an amaryllis *Hippeastrum* anytime soon, it's equally unlikely that the calla lily will become *Zantedeschia* in our collective consciousness. Using correct Latin names should be one of your long-term goals, but as long as you grow this wonderful winter-flowering bulb, you can call it what you please.

GROWING. There is nothing at all tricky about getting a huge calla plant to produce a fragrant succession of flowers all winter long. This plant enjoys sunny windows, but will still flower in a slightly shady spot. The one thing that the calla absolutely must have is copious amounts of water, but this is part of what makes them fun to grow.

In their marshy South African habitats, callas (*Zantedeschia aetheopica*) often grow taller than most people, and the ones you pot in your house will easily reach three feet tall and several feet across. If you have space issues that need to be worked out, do it before you grow these plants because they won't fit on a little wall shelf in the hall. Callas are the big girls of your wintertime season, and they should be given the room they need to really shine.

Dormant calla rhizomes are planted vertically with their tips poking out of the soil. Use a deep pot and leave room at the top for adding compost later. Water at this time to settle the soil, but wait until growth begins before you really wade in with the liquid this plant loves so well. During this period, be sure to keep the pot slightly cool and out of bright light.

Once the large, arrowhead-shaped leaves begin to unroll, place your pot of calla lilies into a bowl of water so that the bottom is always wet. Begin feeding with ordinary indoor plant fertilizer like the granulated types that are mixed with water.

Unlike some tender bulbs, callas bloom better when heavily fertilized, so it's a good idea to establish a regular feeding routine. In an old plastic milk or juice container, mix one gallon of water with half the amount of fertilizer ordinarily recommended. After mixing, mark the gallon container carefully so that no one mistakes it for (blue) Kool-Aid, and use this mixture for fertilizing your callas. If you decided that every Friday is fertilizer day, simply pour about one cup of the already prepared mixture into the bowl of water that serves as your calla's own personal marsh. This will soak up into the pot and feed the plant.

One day in February, you'll notice that a different sort of leaf is starting to unfurl. The curved white part of the calla

lily is actually a specialized leaf called a spathe, and the true flowers are the tiny fuzzies on the yellow spike inside. As you examine this astonishing thing, you'll notice that the calla also has a very

pleasing, faint perfume that's captivating.

DORMANCY. The calla lily opera is a full-length show, and your star needs to rest up after her performance. Treat callas like the rest of your South African bulbs and encourage summer dormancy. Stop fertilizing your callas in April, but continue to water them until the middle of summer. Then allow the water in the bowl to dry up. Let the foliage decline and dry, but be forewarned that this part is not pretty. Keep your calla in an out-of-the-way place during this stage. When everything has withered, cut off all growth at soil level, and store the pot with a lid on top in a warm, dry, dark place.

By autumn the soil will be powdery dry, and if you want to create more pots of callas for the next blooming season, you can pull the rhizomes and divide them among several pots. (Unlike clivias, callas usually bloom the season after division.) It is not necessary to divide your callas if you choose not to; just leave them in their pots and begin watering when they sprout up in late autumn.

outside for a little fresh air. (But don't move these plants outdoors until late spring temperatures are sure not to drop below 55°F.) Begin slowly acclimating the plants to outdoor life by placing them outside in a shady, protected spot for no longer than two hours. Increase their exposure by two hours a day until one week has passed; by then it should be safe for them to stay out indefinitely.

Leave the pots in a protected spot (such as the back wall of a porch or a shady covered patio), and be alert for strong winds, which can tear their leaves. If you move tender bulbs outside in summer, keep them in their pots and follow the individual directions for inducing dormancy periods.

TILL NEXT YEAR

Growing and learning about tender bulbs is a big step toward creating a glorious indoor garden. Although they have their own ways and wiles, the enormous plus of warm-weather dormancy makes tender bulbs a natural choice for people who concentrate on outdoor gardens during the summer months. Keep in mind that tenders are also great for folks who travel in summer, because no one's going to have to be hired to watch after those sleeping beauties. Finally, enjoy these unusual plants not only for their beauty, but also as a reminder that there is a fascinating floral world just waiting to be explored.

☙ LEFT *Unlike many other indoor bulbs, oxalis needs a very warm, sunny window. This pink-flowered type stays in bloom for months and is dormant in summer.*

CHAPTER THREE house-plants: filling *in the* gaps

HOUSEPLANTS FOR HEDONISTS

THE REVIVAL OF THE OUTDOOR GARDEN has spilled over into the renewal of the indoor garden. Growing great indoor plants is fun again, and there's no time like the present to enjoy a plant fling or two. Jazz up your house with jasmine, flip out over ferns, or treat yourself to cheap and cheerful primroses by the grocery cartful. Forget about those old African violets dying a slow death on the shelf, and banish thoughts of snake plants smashed against the venetian blinds. Houseplants have never looked more fresh.

A whole new generation has taken up indoor gardening as yet another creative aspect of today's lively domestic scene. There's a fashionable new world of houseplants offered in this

❧ LEFT *Pots of primroses peek out from under an entryway bench. Purchased from the grocery store, these plants are perfect company for forced bulbs.*

chapter—and they're especially fun when approached with a little hedonism in mind.

Although a great deal of this book is devoted to hardy and tender bulbs, no indoor garden is complete without additional horticultural diversions. Filling out the homescape with well-selected plants is as fun (and necessary) as accessorizing a new suit.

Pairing off plants often brings out hidden qualities, and creative matchmaking is one of the greatest pleasures of the indoor garden. Two large amaryllis bulbs waiting to break dormancy can look a little bare all by their lonesome. But place a small pelargonium 'Metallica' next to them, and its rust-red and medium green leaves suddenly bring out the brown, red, and green colors of those resting bulbs. An indoor trellis covered with bird's-foot ivy can sit in a corner with a gathering of spring bulbs at its base. And alternating pots of golden-leaved plectranthus can accentuate the sunny yellow of forced 'Tête à Tête' daffodils.

☙ LEFT *Pelargonium 'Metallica' adds a feeling of liveliness next to the big bulbs of* Amaryllis *'Rilona,' in the process of being water forced.*

P l a n t   P r i m e r

FICUS

The rubber tree is native to the wet, tropical jungles of Asia. But even when potted as an indoor plant, it tends to be as sturdy as an old rubber boot. *Ficus elastica* 'Black Prince' (at right) thrives in semi-shade, in ordinary potting soil with little or no fertilizing. You can also let the soil dry out completely before watering again.

This plant can deal with all sorts of neglect when it comes to soil, water, and fertilizer, and if you plan to keep yours to a reasonable size, don't spend too much time being nice to it. Rubber trees have been known to grow to enormous, unwieldy sizes, but this characteristic is easy to control. No matter how gnarley the roots become, or how far they dangle out of the container, resist all urges to give your rubber tree a more spacious pot. If you pot up a size or two, your rubber tree will respond to your hospitality by making a bid for the entire family

room. In this case, smaller really is better.

Sometimes rubber trees can attract scale or mealy bugs; treat these pesky critters as prescribed in "How to Pick and Be Picky" on page 96. Also, if you see brown patches on the leaves, it may be a sign that the plant needs to be moved out of the hot midday sun. Because large, glossy leaves are what rubber trees are all about, be sure to keep them looking their best by giving them an occasional shower. Nothing will diminish the glory of your indoor garden faster than a dusty rubber tree.

A rubber tree makes a robust statement on its own, but you may want to add a few bulbs as they come into bloom. The sculptural beauty of 'Black Prince' makes an elegant companion to a soldierly row of deep red tulips. The tulip cultivar 'Oscar' (one of the bright red tulips inexpensively available in the pre-forced market) accents the red of the rubber tree's emerging leaves and creates quite an event from plant elements that could otherwise be overlooked as solo items.

THE RIGHT PLANT IN
THE RIGHT PLACE

Don't despair if your house isn't blessed with "ideal" growing conditions. There are plants that require plenty of sunlight and those that do not. Some houseplants crave warmth, while others prefer temperatures on the chilly side. The happy news is that there is a perfect plant for nearly every place.

Low Light. The most frequent complaints about houseplants usually come from the apartment dweller who receives only a few hours of sun each day. If you have an east-facing window that gets no direct light after 10 A.M., however, you can still grow plants.

The robust, black-leaved rubber tree (*Ficus elastica* 'Black Prince') is a handsome addition to any room. Kin to the common green rubber tree, this plant has glossy purplish-black leaves that are covered with bright red sheaths before they unfurl. Match this with a dark glazed pot and you have a knockout houseplant that requires very little light. (Just don't tell anyone

◈ LEFT *Abutilon, also known as flowering maple or parlor maple, is an excellent plant for shady corners.*

that you picked up the plant and pot at the mall or home-repair superstore.)

High Heat. Another supposedly impossible plant scenario is the tiny, hot, dry apartment with only one window that you wouldn't want to block with a large plant. No problem—place a small copper tray on the windowsill and add several tiny pots of succulents. These fascinating plants are native to inhospitable regions of the world where the desertlike conditions are just like those in your living room.

The most widely available succulents have fat, juicy leaves for storing water. They appear in many colors and are arranged in a fascinating variety of shapes. Some succulents look like miniature blue-gray trees, others look like shiny maroon cabbages, and still others look like tiny, craggy apple trees in full flower. Conventional wisdom has it that succulents don't

∾ RIGHT *This tray of heat-loving succulents thrives in a sunny, hot window.*

GERANIUM

The plants we commonly call geraniums properly belong to the genus *Pelargonium.* They love a hot, dry house. The more familiar types, like the one pictured at right, can have big, cheerful clusters of pink, red, or white flowers. Usually bedded out into the garden in summer, they may be dug up, potted, and brought inside before the first frost arrives. They will bloom indoors in late winter when kept on a sunny window and fertilized once a week.

More unusual geraniums can be found among the dainty and intriguing scented varieties, like the one pictured at left. These plants release perfumes when

∾ LEFT *Scented geraniums prefer slightly dry soil and require very little fertilizing.*

their leaves are crushed. They're relatively simple to grow, and the foliage comes in a delightful array of fragrances including apple, peppermint, nutmeg, lemon, rose, and even Old Spice aftershave. Leaves from scented geraniums make a wonderful addition to bath water.

Scented geraniums are an old-fashioned treat for indoor gardens. These South African plants were first brought into cultivation in England in 1632, and

soon became wildly popular pot plants in both cottages and grander houses. By 1800, scented geraniums assumed economic importance when those with rose-scented leaves became a successful field crop in Turkey. The oil produced from their leaves was processed as a less expensive substitute for attar of roses.

A row of scented geraniums in mismatched pots has a certain informal, cottagelike appeal. Their rounded or lobed leaves and mounded forms look great with simple pots of forced grape hyacinths or smaller irises like 'George.' For a more formal look, substitute a lemon-scented geranium clipped into a classic lollipop topiary. (Just remember to temporarily relocate your geraniums from their unusual hot spots while the forced bulbs are around—forced bulbs do not survive long in hot windows.)

Pots of scented geraniums should be turned regularly to prevent the plants from leaning one way into the sun and becoming misshapen. If a particular branch becomes too long or spoils the shape of the plant, simply snip it off. Scented geraniums can survive even drastic prunings.

bloom, but this is simply not true. If your place is truly as hot and dry as a desert, echeveria, a beautiful gray sculptured succulent, will suddenly begin to extend a fleshy stem that winds

along the windowsill as it grows. Within a few weeks this stem sprouts beautiful rosy flowers that last for well over a month. These are later replaced by baby plants, which can be plucked right off the stem and potted. Succulents are simple to grow, respond happily to neglect, and serve as exciting reminders that even the desert occasionally bursts into bloom.

When it comes to companion plants, remember that forced hardy bulbs will not survive in your succulents' preferred environment. Just one morning on a hot, dry windowsill and the cheeriest daffodils will melt like candles. The tender bulb bowiea (see page 72), however, looks and feels right at home with heat-loving succulents. The airiness of bowiea's twining vines will not block your window as a bulky plant would, and an attractive stick trellis will support the vines and add a graceful touch of

∾ LEFT *Happy succulents may burst out with astonishingly strange flowers if the conditions are right.*

verticality to the horizontal tray of succulents.

Cool Conditions. At the other end of the temperature spectrum is the cool environment. If you live in such conditions and your plants tend to suffer and die, you may have simply purchased the wrong plants. Both hardy bulbs and most tender bulbs stay in bloom much longer in a cool room, so look for companion plants, such as jasmine, that also like these temperatures. Many commercial growers feature a cool greenhouse with plants that thrive where it may drop as low as 50°F at night.

Shady Corners. Almost every dwelling has one location that needs a bit of cheering up. Many city apartments have dark kitchens and bathrooms, and even the largest, most sun-filled house has at least one gloomy corner. To make these areas more appealing, choose a plant that

∾ RIGHT *This succulent bloomed for weeks in a hot, dry window. When summer arrives, it will serve as a failure-proof potted plant on a sunny terrace.*

Plant Primer

COLEUS

Until recently, any mention of the word coleus was enough to make a plant connoisseur shudder. For unknown reasons, this group of shade-loving plants had fallen out of favor and even picked up the derisive nickname of "barbershop plant." Thankfully, these brightly colored plants have been dusted off and returned to the horticultural limelight they rightly deserve.

The reason for their renewed popularity is logical: coleus has spectacularly gorgeous leaves and is singularly easy to grow. If you keep coleuses out of the sun, well-watered and fertilized, they will gratefully brighten up even the darkest corner of your home.

A wide variety of coleuses are now available in nurseries, in greenhouses—

LEFT This stunning coleus dominates a north-facing window, leaving only a little breathing room for a plate of acorns in water.

and for those with a good eye—on grocery shelves, too. Almost everyone recognizes the coleus with small, scalloped burgundy leaves with green highlights. There is also a variety with small, stunning black leaves and green mottling. Beyond their low-maintenance cultivation requirements, coleuses are versatile plants that pair well with a range of other plants and bulbs.

A pot bursting with a large apricot-and-light-green coleus placed near a pale orange amaryllis 'Rilona' will chase away those dead-of-winter blues. A black-and-green coleus partnered with forced scarlet tulips is simple and shockingly beautiful. Add a few interesting ivy cultivars and a fern or two to the aforementioned mix, and create an entire indoor garden that shimmers from your shadiest corner.

Coleus is a snap to keep neat and tidy. To train your coleus or make it bushier, use sharp scissors to cut back stems just above where a leaf sprouts. Two stems will eventually sprout at every cut. If you want your coleus to drape dramatically over the side of its pot, keep cutting off upward growing stems to achieve a trailing effect. For a rounder, fuller shape, routinely cut as many stems as possible to encourage sprouting of multiple branches. If you have one of the larger-growing coleus, you can even create a lollipop topiary shape. When you're attempting this style of pruning, keep in mind that the stems tend to be a bit weak, so be sure to tie the main trunk to a supporting stick with twine.

enjoys low light levels to create a little bit of excitement in an otherwise dreary space.

If your dark corner is a windowless kitchen, try a small pot of white-and-green variegated ivy to add a bit of life and speckled color under the counter light. For that air shaft in the bathroom of your apartment, you might want something a little more exotic. Keep your eyes open for the smaller, inexpensive shade-loving orchids that keep their blossoms intact for months. These compact plants adore the extra humidity from your showers and easily lend quite an air of luxury to your home.

In a dwelling with a bit more space, requisition an unwanted dark corner for your own personal territory. A comfortable chair, a small side table, a reading lamp, and a pot of primulas is enough to stake your claim. Or if you prefer, consider one of the smaller begonias, a cyclamen, or even a pot of brightly colored coleus.

There is a delectable coleus to decorate any room, and they're now available in black, lime green, ruby red, apricot, creamy yellow, and colorful patterns and combinations. These shade lovers—once relegated to spaces behind the blinds in barbershop windows or doomed to languish in the gloom of back halls—have made a fashionable comeback in a very big way. And even if their prices have risen during their recent ascent in popularity, a chartreuse coleus is still a better accessory for your new gray couch than a tiny tapestry pillow.

No Light, No Problem. Once you've seen how a fashionably colored coleus can light up the shadows of your house, you may want to consider a few other shade-loving plants. If you think practically, there are many shady places on earth (think: the undercanopy of a jungle) that

RIGHT *Unusual begonias are always treasured finds. Keep them away from direct sun, and fertilize regularly.*

Plant Primer

JASMINE

One of the most evocative perfumes to waft from a flower is available only to those who like their houses chilly. Both the twining (*Jasminum polyanthum*) and shrubby types (*J. humile* clones and cultivars) positively love a cool house. In fact, if these woody houseplants experience temperatures much over 65°F, they simply won't come into bloom. Keep jasmine plants in as much light as possible, but not in hot, direct sun. A bright north-facing window will work, or you can place these little temptresses on a table far away from radiators or the fireplace.

As the sprays of small white flowers start to open, keep the plants well watered and fertilized. As more and more buds appear and pop open, jasmine's tropical scent bestows a sweet-smelling reprieve from the bleakness of winter.

If you're able, place your jasmine outdoors when warm weather arrives. You may lightly prune the plant at this time without compromising next winter's blooms, and regular fertilizing will spur new growth. A position in bright shade suits jasmine best, and don't forget to bring the plant back inside before the frost in autumn.

Climbing jasmine scampers and curls in a very graceful way, but the bottom of the plant tends to look like a tumble of green. This problem is easily solved by placing a pot or two of the shiny green rosettes of tender veltheimia (see page 79) around your jasmine. The tall pink stem of the potted bulb absolutely lights up against the dark green of jasmine, and since veltheimia adores exactly the same low light and cool temperatures as jasmine, this marriage is nothing short of perfect. Furthermore, as veltheimia has no discernable scent, it won't compete with the exotic fragrance of the jasmine.

are lush and green and bursting with vegetation.

North-facing windows are ideal spots to display colorful blooms of forced bulbs or a little collection of bushy ferns. Sprays of fern fronds are gorgeous next to pots of daffodils, crocuses, or tulips, and add a softness that bulb foliage usually doesn't exhibit. Also, long after your bulbs have faded, the ferns will carry on, unrolling and unfolding new greenery to decorate your own private indoor jungle.

Parlor-gardening Victorians loved ferns. Illustrations of interiors from that era show enormous terrariums made especially to house precious fern specimens, and some parlors even had large aquariums built into the scheme. Another fern-protecting device—actually the precursor to the terrarium—was a fragile glass box called a Wardian case, which was usually displayed on a delicately designed iron table. As

pteridomania (the fern craze) reached manic levels, intricate fern displays (and all their fragile

☙ RIGHT *Primrose and butterfly-like cyclamen flowers prefer a cool, shady spot to produce their best winter blooms.*

protective glass) put a considerable damper on any kind of indoor horseplay.

Modern indoor gardeners—especially those living with energetic toddlers, budding

ballerinas, or enthusiastic dogs—will be happy to learn that many ferns grow happily outside terrariums and Wardian cases as long as there is some way to add the moisture they crave. A copper tray filled with pebbles and water sitting on a radiator will do the job, as will bowls of water placed near an assortment of potted ferns. A daily spritz or two from a mister should also add enough humidity to keep everyone happy. If a particular fern looks withered or is producing new fronds that are dried out, try moving that pot to the bathroom or kitchen where there tends to be higher humidity.

If you know that your house is too hot and dry for ferns, you can still add a nice touch of no-light, low-maintenance greenery by growing sprigs of ivy in vases of water. Ivy has no objections to this hydroponic method and will look fresh forever, growing new leaves and

❧ LEFT *A shady bathroom corner is lit up with sprigs of rooting variegated ivy and the speckled leaves of a begonia.*

STAGHORN FERN

The staghorn fern appears as macho as a green thing can possibly be. When correctly grown on a piece of bark and hung from the wall or ceiling, it looks exactly like the plant world equivalent of a rack of trophy antlers.

Staghorn ferns (*Platycerium* spp.) are native to the tropics. They grow on the sides or in the forks of large trees, but because they are epiphytic, they perch on other plants without being parasitic. Staghorn foliage is dimorphic (having two different shapes). The branching, antler-like leaves serve as showy reproductive units while the flat, inverted, plate-shaped leaves attach the plant to the tree. The flat leaves are sterile but very important—they trap water and tree debris to nourish the plant.

Staghorn ferns are available from good greenhouses and are always purchased mounted on their bark home and ready for hanging. There are almost twenty species in the genus, and while some are larger than others, they're so slow to increase in size that you can trust that whatever specimen you buy won't take over the entire room anytime soon.

When growing staghorns, keep in mind that they must be watered often—and that you don't want the water to drip down onto your sofa from above. Either remove the fern from the wall before watering (the bigger the fern, the bigger the job) or hang it someplace where a bowl can be positioned to catch the drips. As staghorns absorb water through their leaves, they also love a good misting. Because this plant revels in low-light areas, the perfect position for your staghorn just might be a wall over the shower.

draping itself artistically off the edge of a shelf, or from the top ledge of a shady window. If you want to try something a bit fancier with ivy, look for variegated cultivars ('Goldheart' or 'Glacier') or those with interesting leaves ('Asterisk' or 'Irish Lace'). Special ivy greenhouses stock hundreds of cultivars, and you can accumulate quite a collection of ivies without ever purchasing an ounce of potting soil.

If you long for a few flowers in your shady house, consider begonias as an old-fashioned way to add interesting foliage and oddly sweet blooms to your plant combinations. The genus *Begonia* is large (with over a thousand species) and warm-hearted (mostly tropical and subtropical), with enough variation among its members to fascinate the most jaded of gardeners. Some

begonias have shiny leaves spotted with silver, while others have matte green leaves completely covered in dramatic red whiskers. Many begonias remain on the petite side for years, while others may grow to five feet tall. The best are

❧ LEFT *A small forest of ferns requires very little light but needs frequent watering and misting.* ❧ RIGHT *Begonias need warmth and a moist atmosphere, but care should be taken not to overwater.*

purchased from a good greenhouse or specialty grower, but you may spot a real beauty winking at you from an ordinary grocery store display. Begonias like the same conditions as ferns, and the dainty variety *Begonia fuchsiodes* (syn. *B. foliosa* var. *miniata*) is a stunner when displayed with cascading fronds of maidenhair ferns and a few forced lilies of the valley.

∾ ABOVE *This collection of scented geraniums sits on a sunny bathroom shelf. The aromatic leaves can be added to hot bathwater for a soothing scent.*

HOW TO PICK AND BE PICKY

The houseplants you buy will probably come from local greenhouses or plant stores—usually as an impulse purchase when the plants are in

Plant Primer

Pretty in Pots

The rule of thumb when it comes to plant containers is simply that you should please yourself. Great pots are a major part of enjoying the indoor garden, and there's no better way to reward yourself for horticultural achievements.

Once you fall for a plant and bring it home, you might as well dress it up a bit, too. The best way to pep up any indoor garden is to have a great selection of pots on hand.

Keep your eyes open for unusual pot-purchasing opportunities. Flea markets, craft stores, home improvement centers, and yard sales occasionally yield terrific pots. When purchasing any second-hand containers, good plant hygiene requires soaking pots in bleach and water before using.

Even the most mundane ivy cutting can become a spectacular little plant when draped from a matte-black pot. A row of brightly colored glazed pots is perfect for displaying collections of scented geraniums, and a pink blooming begonia

(*Begonia fuchsioides*, syn. *B. foliosa* var. *miniata*) looks very sweet in a pale blue pot. Confetti-colored primulas (available on the cheap every winter in grocery stores) become suitable gifts when repotted into traditional terra-cotta pots, especially when packed as a set in a small wooden clementine crate. If you go for a more modern look, inexpensive brass cachepots perfectly complement the

spiky leaves and electric-blue cascading flowers of queen's tears (*Billbergia nutans*), and create a bold, exotic mood.

Some indoor decors demand simple displays of plants, while a wild exuberance fits well in others. An all-white living room may call for a row of white pots with matching ferns, or a single scarlet pot with an enormous rubber tree. An Arts-and-Crafts-era house may look best with an indoor jungle of plants, bulbs, and vines that echoes the garden style of that period, while a 1950s retro decor just cries out for a large tropical statement.

their prime growing stage and looking fabulous. The big challenge comes in keeping them looking as gorgeous and healthy as they did the day you bought them.

Part of the secret to raising great indoor plants involves bug warfare. Many outdoor gardeners take an organic approach and don't mind a chewed leaf or two outside. But houseplants are already forced into an artificial existence as a result of being potted indoors, and even the most easygoing outdoor gardeners look after inside plants more carefully to avoid infestations throughout their collection.

The first line of defense against bugs is to examine every plant *before* it comes into your house. Look for fine white webs (evidence of spider mites), tiny white dots of cotton (mealybugs), little green bugs (aphids), or squishy brown dots (scale). Resist the urge to buy any plant with these creatures on them or you risk passing the bugs to all the plants at home.

∾ LEFT *Scented geraniums can be trained into topiary shapes. Pinch off any stray sprigs that appear at the base or along the trunk, and use scissors to keep the top foliage nicely rounded.* ∾ RIGHT *The tropical American plant* Billbergia nutans *has stiff, slightly toothed leaves. This plant produced graceful blue-and-green flowers a few weeks after the neighboring pink primrose flowers faded.*

If you find yourself on the offensive with any of the above already in residence in your house, persistence is your best weapon. Aphids and spider mites can usually be controlled with sprays of ordinary dishwashing soap. Add about two big drops of soap per pint of water in a sprayer. Place the plant in a sink or tub and spray each leaf and branch thoroughly. Leave the plant for half an hour, then spray it again with a direct stream of cool water to rinse off the soap. Let the plant rest out of direct sun for one day to recu-

ᕦ ABOVE Begonia fuchsioides *(sometimes listed as* B. foliosa *var.* miniata*) makes an unusual addition to any begonia collection.*

perate. Repeat this every two weeks until the bugs are gone.

Scale and mealybugs can be swabbed away with ordinary rubbing alcohol. Place the plant on the kitchen counter where a strong light will help you to spot the enemy. Pour rubbing alcohol into a small dish and dunk five or six cotton swabs in it. Keeping a handful of swabs at the ready in the dish makes the process go a little faster.

Search methodically through your plants and dab away every critter you see. When you see no further signs of bug life, rinse the entire plant in the sink and let it rest out of sunlight for the next day. Repeat in two weeks, which will probably be necessary because both scale and mealybugs are very stubborn.

꙳ RIGHT *If pastel colors aren't for you, look for bold foliage and flowers at a local greenhouse, and pair the plants with wildly colored pots or containers for some indoor excitement.*

TWO SUREFIRE WAYS TO KILL A PLANT

Although bugs may be the main suspects when a plant goes into decline, two other factors often contribute to a houseplant's demise. Plant pam-

pering is one of the great joys of having an indoor garden, but overwatering and overfertilizing will kill a plant faster than anything else.

You can't expect to follow a strictly regimented weekly watering schedule. When the weather outside is cloudy, even indoor plants don't usually need much water, while many sunny days in a row may leave some plants needing a daily dousing. Your own finger pushed into the soil is a better water gauge than any mechanical device or rigid timetable.

Overfeeding a plant is a far more common error than underfeeding. And while some plants like a weekly dose of water-soluble fertilizer, others will respond poorly to this treatment. Forced bulbs, for example, don't need fertilizing at all; some tender bulbs will refuse to bloom if fertilized; and scented geraniums will lose their

∾ LEFT *Gardener Page Dickey keeps a collection of cyclamens and primroses in her cool entryway to welcome her wintertime guests.*

perfumed leaves if overfed. Also, never feed fresh transplants because fertilizer will burn newly emerging roots and can kill the entire plant.

Another sign to cut back on fertilizing is overenthusiastic growth. Overfed plants get floppy, and too much fertilizer also makes a plant attractive to constant hordes of aphids, drawn to the weak, juicy leaves produced from a diet that is too rich.

The best bet for making sure that you don't kill your plants with love is to use the commercially available, water-soluble fertilizers affectionally nicknamed "big blues" (because they tint the water turquoise when dissolved). These are preferred by professionals, but a rank amateur can simply follow the dosages recommended on the package and get outstanding results. Even those who keep their outdoor gardens strictly organic often allow themselves to use these artificial fertilizers indoors. Organic means are almost always preferable, but most totally natural fertilizers have more of the barnyard (manure tea) or low-tide-at-the-seashore (fish emulsion) bouquet than is comfortable within the confines of a small apartment.

PETS IN POTS

Great houseplants are a thriving part of the new and improved indoor garden scene. These pets in pots make lively decorations on windowsills and tabletops, and their cheerful presence complements seasonal hardy and tender bulbs. A small family of interesting houseplants is the first step toward creat-ing your own inside paradise.

twigs and branches: also forced

BRANCHING OUT:
FOLIAGE AND FLOWERS

ORCING HARDY BULBS FOR WINTER ENJOYMENT IS a big deal, but forcing branches to bloom before spring is a small wonder. The act of forcing branches is little

∾ LEFT *These blossoming fruit branches were purchased at the flower market, and will stay in bloom for ten days if kept cool.* ∾ RIGHT *A local arborist provided these apple tree prunings. They don't produce flowers, but are excellent for making indoor trellises.*

more than gathering bare sticks outdoors, bringing them inside, and watching them unfurl their leaves and flowers. It is a beautiful process that quietly reminds us of the unspoken promises of the spring to come.

Hortus Third defines forcing as artificially manipulating plants to grow or bloom before their normal season, adding that "growing in greenhouses is not necessarily forcing; it may only be protection." Houseplants, therefore, cannot be said to be forced, but merely protected. Likewise, tender bulbs that naturally bloom in the Southern Hemisphere's hot winters are not truly forced, but simply protected from our hemisphere's cold winters.

Blooming hardy bulbs in winter, however, is true forcing, as is cutting bare branches and twigs in cold weather and bringing them inside to flower before the arrival of spring. The former activity involves several months of planning and anticipation, while the latter doesn't require much time or effort at all. Forcing branches is a simple technique that may be the easiest midwinter trick in the realm of indoor gardening.

∾ LEFT *These birch branches sprouted long, fuzzy catkins in February when forced on a windowsill.*

THINKING OUTSIDE THE BOX: GATHERING YOUR MATERIAL

The flower and leaf buds on woody plants (think shrubs and trees) are formed during the autumn. In the temperate part of the world, these buds require at least six weeks of cold weather before their dormancy can be successfully broken by forcing indoors. If your frosty weather begins in November, this means that you may start

☙ ABOVE *Bare twigs of corylopsis can be forced to burst into fragrant flower early in the year.*

Branch Primer

Perfect Pairs

Forced branches and forced bulbs are perfect companions. Both keep their flowers longer when temperatures are on the cool side, and all forced bulbs and branches prefer to be kept out of the sun. Pairing these delights of spring couldn't look any more natural and—as long as you don't get too anxious about what is going to bloom when— some wonderful matches may occur. Always keep in mind that part of the fun of forcing is its unpredictability, so look at things as they happen and keep notes on next year's calendar.

The range of possible bulb-branch pairings is staggering. Great yellow wands of forced forsythia look terrific with small pots of shaggy golden 'Rip van Winkle' daffodils. Gather the forsythia into a tall vase and place the 'Rip van Winkle' around its base. You could also try the

very early yellow witch hazel with pots of yellow-cupped winter aconite. All are early forcers and display the bright yellow-gold that seems to be Nature's first call to spring.

If more subtle colors are your preference, pastel blooms of fruit trees look soft and natural with tiny, sky-blue scillas forced in terra-cotta pots. Individual scillas can actually be forced in tiny containers, so if you want to make a series of small, short arrangements of fruit blossoms, you can scatter the little scilla pots on a tabletop among the little vases. Because everything is short, you can use the combination as a long centerpiece running down the middle of the dining table (just make sure that low-burning candles don't scorch the flowers).

∾ RIGHT *If you have forsythia in your garden, prune the shrubs back after they flower in spring. This technique produces very long and graceful stems for next winter's forcing.*

cutting branches for indoor use around the end of January, and you can easily keep bringing them in as late as mid March.

The period from January to March is also the height of the indoor bulb season, and

pots of blooming bulbs and vases of forced branches look terrific together. *Wyman's Gardening Encyclopedia* says that "forcing branches is the favorite indoor sport of growers," but you don't really have to grow much at all to participate in this charming game. Just keep your eyes open, and all sorts of branches for forcing will charm their way into your house.

One of the most popular shrubs for forcing is the omnipresent forsythia. Cut into long switches, its branches are absolutely fetching when arranged like a stop-action fireworks explosion on the piano or coffee table. Another unbeatable forcer is quince, a gray twiggy mass of shrub that produces bright orange-pink flowers. Both these shrubs can be purchased from most garden centers and are no-brainers to grow. Once you get started with this type of forcing, you might find it impossible to resist "branching

∾ LEFT *A tiny twig of* Rhus typhinia '*Laciniata' (cut-leaf sumac) sprouts a feathery leaf when forced.*

out" a bit with other types of garden shrubs.

Many gardeners plant shrubs with the specific intention of forcing a few branches in winter, and as long as the clipping is not over-done, the bushes will still bloom beautifully. If you have room in your garden, you might want to add a witch hazel (*Hamamelis*) for its very early, very frilly yellow flowers, or a redbud (*Cercis*) for the raspberry-purple flowers that cluster close to the stem. The so-called white for-sythia (*Abeliophyllum distichum*) shows off its dainty pale flowers against handsomely dark stems. The tiny, dense rosettes of 'Bridal Wreath' spirea pop open like little white roses when forced, and wands of this branch make great arrangements next to forced hyacinths. Any type of pussy willow will delight the children in your life, but the striking black pussy willow (*Salix*

melanostachys) and its shiny red stems can make anyone gasp. Planting cutting shrubs is a great way to expand your knowledge of less-common plants such as honey-scented fothergilla, while

∾ RIGHT *Small blossoms that look like tiny white roses sprout from sticks of spirea 'Bridal Wreath.' The forced twigs of this shrub look great paired with forced hardy bulbs such as blue hyacinths.*

The Case for the Right Container

Once you've chosen the twigs and branches that you want, the next step is to consider their containers. Sweetly blossoming peach branches just don't pack any punch when jammed down into any old pickle jar. The bottoms of those branches eventually get unsightly in water, so pick something that keeps this little fact of life concealed. An attractive blue-and-white china jug, for example, looks right with those gnarled dark branches, and one solitary cragged branch can lean over the edge in a pleasing manner.

On the other hand, willow branches keep beautifully in water, and you'll be missing half the show if you can't see how

beautifully their white roots wind inside a clear vase.

If you've only been able to cut the tiniest of twigs for your indoor garden, then use the tiniest of containers. Old medicine bottles, often in pale green or blue glass, make great little vases, as do old test tubes with wooden holders. Mixed bud vases are an obvious choice, and if you treat yourself to a carton of those delicious Italian apéritif soft drinks with old-fashioned metal tops, you can make a pretty row of six identical tiny bottles. These look especially good when lined up along the top edge of a kitchen window.

Great big branches need great big vases, but indoor gardeners with curious cats and boisterous kids need to make sure that those urns don't careen off a shelf or flood an entire table top. Tall branches are top-heavy, but you can prevent tipping accidents by filling a large vase half full with sand or rocks before adding water and branches.

also providing lots of interesting forcing materials for your indoor garden.

You don't even need a garden to force branches. You can trade a few potted bulbs with a friend in exchange for branches, or offer to purchase trimmings from the local arborist as he goes about his tree-trimming work in winter.

Weed-filled vacant lots can offer great cuttings. Wild cherry makes tiny, sweet pink flowers on purple wood. Twisted vines of bittersweet, a tangly woody twiner, pop open with little green beads that form along gray corkscrews of stem. Staghorn sumac (*Rhus thyphina*) will force, usually managing to push at least one green leaf from its stubby, fuzzy, antlerlike branch in an amazing feat of weedy will.

∾ RIGHT *The white flowers of early blooming* Abeliophyllum distichum *have led some to misname this shrub white forsythia.* Abeliophyllum *is easy to force and a perfect match for black pussy willow.*

When gathering branches for forcing, just be careful not to trespass on someone else's property, collect plant material from protected areas, or damage any tree or shrub—yours or someone else's. Although natural places may look peaceful, calm, and deserted, every public field, wetland, and woodland is truly an endangered ecosystem and should be treated with the utmost respect.

You can also ask permission from your landlord to cut a few twigs from outside bushes. Almost any house or apartment building—even those with only foundation plantings—can yield a few twigs for cutting without detracting from the landscape effect.

Ordinary pieris, the evergreen shrub sometimes called lily-of-the-valley shrub or (incorrectly) andromeda, is a very common landscape plant with a surprising secret life. Although pieris looks a bit lonely and drab outside in winter, when you cut a few twigs in February and bring them inside, their hidden beauty is unlocked. When placed in water, the evergreen leaves perk right up, and scores of pale pinkish white flowers slowly sprout from the tips of the

∽ LEFT *The cut bright yellow branches of weeping willow make graceful wands of leaves and eventually fill a vase with winding roots.*

BRANCH-FORCING TIMETABLE (ZONE 5 CONDITIONS)

Shrub	*Blooms when cut at end of January*	*Blooms when cut in mid March*
FORSYTHIA	third week of February	last week of March
WITCH HAZEL	mid February	blooming outside
REDBUD	early March	end of March
WHITE FORSYTHIA	late February	third week of March
SPIREA	early March	first week of April
PUSSY WILLOW	mid February	blooming outside
BITTERSWEET	mid March	end of March
WILD CHERRY	mid February	end of March
STAGHORN SUMAC	late February	end of March
PIERIS	end of February	third week of March
FRUIT TREES	early March	end of March
MAPLE	end of February	end of March
WEEPING WILLOW	end of February	end of March

branches and tumble down from the stems.

As an added treat, the lowly pieris has a wonderful fragrance rarely noticed when this shrub is relegated to its usual role of guardian of the dryer vent. The flowers and fragrance will last many happy weeks indoors, and might forever alter your perception of these overlooked bushes.

SEE THE FOREST
THROUGH THE TREES

Most tree branches can also be snipped and brought inside for leafing out and blooming. Fruit trees have wonderful blossoms, and even the tiniest patio peach tree won't miss two or

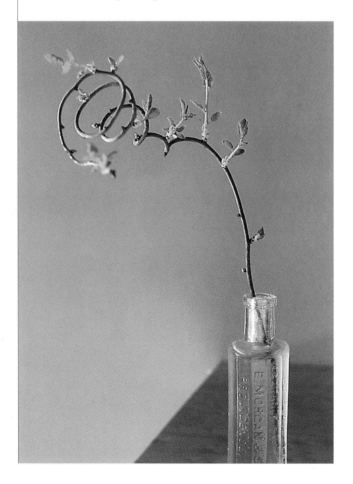

three six-inch twigs. These cragged sticks produce deep pink flowers, while apple twigs have large, almost white flowers. Crabapple twigs are smoother, more graceful, and usually make pretty, medium-pink flowers, although the blossom color can vary greatly from variety to variety. Somewhat surprisingly, the elegant white flowers of pear trees are not suitable indoor additions. If you've ever stuck your nose in pear blossoms, you'll never forget the stench of fish that wafts from those beauties like a bad joke.

Ordinary "yard trees" also have interesting branches to force. Sugar maples make very fancy chartreuse tassels, and red maples create bright scarlet asterisks along their gray branches. Birch trees produce long, fuzzy catkins that look especially great when the tiny new leaves emerge

⮌ LEFT Bittersweet is one of the more sculptural twigs to force. Look in vacant lots for tangles, and carefully unwrap them for unrivaled indoor shapes. ⮌ RIGHT This off-beat arrangement of tchotchkes and forced branches is yet another way to make the most of off-season blooms.

like flecks of green against the flat lace of the branches. Weeping willow trees make wonderfully drooping chartreuse switches that can be put in a vase on top of a bookshelf to gracefully "weep" all the way down to the floor.

A GENTLE UNFURLING

Unlike forced bulbs, forced branches almost happen by themselves. After the required six weeks of cold weather, you can begin to snip branches and bring them indoors. In most areas, you can plan a nice meander around the dormant garden, a bundled-up walk in the woods, or a daring daylight raid on the abandoned lot down the street during the traditional "January thaw," which usually occurs in the mid to late part of the month.

If you're in the middle of a terrible cold snap or deep blizzard, don't bother to cut branches—they force better when cut on a warm

✎ LEFT *Three sticks of forced forsythia, a Moroccan jug, and some blue paint transform a boring corner into an exotic, eye-catching winter scene.*

Making the Most of Branches

When you first force branches, you will undoubtedly be enchanted by the process but a bit bewildered by what to do with the product. Choosing the most flattering container is important, but displaying branches effectively can make the difference between a great display and a bunch of sticks in a vase.

Some tree branches make fascinating blossoms, but as a rule they have less than graceful woody parts. Red maple (sometimes called swamp maple) has rather awkward twigs tipped with wonderful, fuzzy red blossoms. Pick a quirky vase for this type of branch and surround it with some of your most sentimental keepsakes. Arrange branch, vase, and objects like a small altar to mark the arrival of spring, and suddenly, a funny-looking branch achieves a soft beauty.

Another trick for displaying forced branches is to place them against a dark surface or in front of a mirror. A dark background will help silhouette a simple arrangement against a wall and emphasize the stark beauty of a few blossoms on a branch. If you want to create an illusion of fullness, place an arrangement in front of a mirror where everything will be reflected. This is a trick of the trade employed by experienced floral designers, but one that any amateur can use.

day, and the later in winter that you bring things inside, the faster they will bloom. Branches cut in January will take anywhere from two and a half weeks to a month to unfurl, while those harvested as late as mid-March may open in one or two weeks. Cutting a few twigs every weekend will ensure a show of many—and varied—acts.

Once you return to the house with your cut twigs, fill the tub with tepid water and submerge the branches for a gentle two-hour soak. This will moisten and loosen the bud scales. After the bath, fill vases to the brim with room-temperature water, trim at least one inch off the stems, and arrange them in their containers.

BRANCHING OUT

Forcing branches is your opportunity to see how a leaf unlocks itself from wood, and how a sweet little flower unfolds from a dull, dead stick. Enjoying the process makes the visual feast even more delectable, so don't cheat yourself by trying to beat time. This quiet little show is usually overlooked outdoors during the riot of spring, but as winter quietly fades, you have it all to yourself.

ᴗ LEFT *Don't overlook evergreen shrubs when collecting branches for forcing.* Pieris japonica, *thrilled to be out of the cold, produces masses of sweetly scented flowers.*

CHAPTER FIVE cuttings:

new beginnings

MORE PLANTS FOR LESS MONEY

THIS SMALL CODA OF A CHAPTER DEALS with a fact of gardening life that holds true whether you have two acres of flowers outside or three pots of plants inside. When it comes to building plant collections, most gardeners swing wildly between being embarrassingly greedy and

ॐ LEFT *Young 'Bronze Baby' phormiums stand in lines under the watch of a drooping calla lily leaf.* ॐ RIGHT *Ipomoea 'Blackie' cuttings are easily increased in the winter months by rooting them in water.*

incredibly generous. It is not unusual for a gardener to purchase the last 'Bronze Baby' phormium available in the entire county, yet the following year, divide it and make enough new

plants for every friend who had ever desired one of their own. Gardeners adore having plants that no one else has, but they also delight in sharing them with friends. Simple plant propagation is an easy, cost-free way to increase the number of plants you have, and to indulge both acquisitiveness and munificence in one fell swoop.

WHAT ROOTS WHEN, AND HOW TO MAKE IT HAPPEN

There are many books devoted entirely to growing seedlings and cuttings, and nursery professionals have extensive training in the art of plant propagation. But this rewarding activity can often be accomplished by the willing amateur with very simple techniques and tools. The elementary tips listed here will allow you to begin

☙ LEFT *Begonia leaves easily root in water and may be planted in moisture-retaining soil. Keep them out of hot, sunny windows.*

indulging in the pleasures of plant propagation. **Tender Bulbs.** If a friend has admired the bowiea that twined and climbed around your living room window, you can split off one of its bulbs when the group becomes too crowded for the pot. Wait until the vines die back in early summer (signifying that the bulbs are in their dormant state), then simply tap the plant out of the pot, break off one bulb, and pot it up (see page 72) for your friend. The tender bulb melasphaerula can likewise be shared, as it produces little black bulbils along its leaves. Pick these off just as the leaves finish withering in late spring, and pot them up (see page 75). Increasing your stock of these and other unusual tender bulbs is not only easy, but allows you to share with your indoor gardening pals.

Some of the plants in this book, however, are not easily propagated. If you try to

⌘ RIGHT *Willows and ivy, perfect companions on this north-facing window ledge, root easily in water.*

divide your clivia, you'll end up with two clivias that sulk without blooming for several years. Clivias like to be crowded in their pots, so if you decide that you want another plant to match the

one you have, it's better to go out and buy one— then they'll both bloom next winter.

Hardy Bulbs. Increasing forced bulbs is a rather complicated effort, so they're traditionally tossed on the compost heap before they can reproduce. Forcing wears out tulips, daffodils, and other hardy bulbs to such an extent that you'd need to coddle them for many years before they would rejuvenate and multiply. Profession- als can accomplish this (though they rarely

∾ ABOVE *Nasturtiums and plectranthus make a cheerful rooting gallery in a warm but shaded window.*
∾ RIGHT *Plectranthus, a desirable but not hardy garden plant, can be brought inside during winter. It roots easily in water, and can be increased for next year's enjoyment.*

SCENTED GERANIUM

To propagate scented geraniums, begin with a healthy, bushy plant that won't mind a light pruning. Using a clean, very sharp knife, cut off three-inch-long pieces from the mother plant right above a leaf. Professionals insist that scissors should never be used for making cuttings because they smash the delicate stems and cause propagation failure. The pros also say that any time of year—except June and July—is fine for making scented geranium cuttings. Carefully pull off the bottom leaves from each cutting, making sure that there are at least four healthy green leaves left intact, and lay your cuttings on a clean plate.

Although most cuttings are not allowed to wilt, some nursery professionals allow their scented geranium cuttings

to wilt a bit while they are exposed to air for about ten hours. Many believe that this helps prevent damping off, a fungus condition that causes cuttings and new seedlings to suddenly topple over and die. After this rest period, insert the bottom

part of each cutting into a dish of perlite (a rooting medium available at any plant store), water well, and place in a warm (70°F) spot out of the sun. Water with room-temperature water to restore the cuttings to perkiness. (After the initial planned wilt, droopiness is not a good thing.) Firm the perlite around the cuttings because contact between cutting and medium promotes good roots.

Avoid placing scented geranium babies under glass or wrapping them in plastic bags to promote a moist atmosphere. These plants prefer everything to stay slightly on the dry side, and unlike most other plant cuttings, they don't like to be misted.

After two weeks, gently lift a cutting (with the pointed end of a wooden plant marker) to see if any tiny roots have started to appear. If not, replace the plant and try moving it to a warmer spot. Keep the baby plant warm and watered. When new growth appears, gradually move it closer to a sunny window until it can enjoy full sun without wilting.

bother) but for the rest of us, it's better to simply buy more bulbs next fall. If you want to share bulbs, you might remember who fell in love with your 'Orange Queen' narcissus and buy an extra dozen bulbs for them.

Houseplants. On a far cheerier note, there's nothing easier than rooting that expensive coleus you bought last summer. Coleus belongs to the happily increasing mint family and can be propagated anytime year-round. Snip off a four-inch end of a stem, cutting cleanly just above a leaf. Pick off the bottom leaves and place the stem in water. Cuttings put in jars of water out of direct sunlight soon make beautiful kaleidoscopes in every window. The coleus leaves stay fresh and crisp, and as soon as the roots begin to snake around the jar, the cuttings can be transplanted. Simply put a layer

of soil in a small pot, and holding the plant upright, gently drape the roots on top. Add more soil until the plant stands upright, firm the soil, and water well.

Plectranthus, also in the mint family, can be rooted and potted in exactly the same way as coleus. One mother plant produces many

✿ RIGHT *A desirable red-whiskered begonia was successfully propagated by rooting this leaf in water and transplanting it into soil.*

offspring, and periodic trimming helps to keep the plant in shape. Ivy kept in water will also eventually root and can be transplanted into pots if you want. Just follow the same treatment as you would for coleus.

The self-sufficient succulents don't require much help at all to increase. When these dry-heat-loving plants occasionally shed one or two of their juicy little leaves during the winter, simply resist the urge to tidy up and you'll see the most amazing thing. Place the dropped leaves on a plate, and after several weeks, almost every one will miraculously sprout tiny roots without the addition of soil or water. Once several hairlike roots appear, place the leaf on the surface of soil in a pot and a new succulent plant

will grow. Once you start propagating succulents, you'll quickly discover why one of the most common plants from this group is known as mother-of-thousands.

The large, stately succulent *Agave ameri-*

∾ LEFT *An agave youngster and several succulent offspring rest in the hot sun. Visible roots and a small plant sprout can be seen emerging from the unpotted leaf perched on the stone at the right.* ∾ RIGHT *This apricot-flowering succulent, nicknamed mother-of-thousands, produces scores of baby plants that can be repotted and given to friends.*

Inside to Outside in Two Easy Steps

Around the time when the weather outside starts looking great, the garden inside may start looking a bit ragged. Long months indoors are tough on everyone, and even the most well-adjusted indoor plants relish a fresh-air break.

Whatever you do, don't simply take a perfectly happy clivia off the piano and put it out on the patio. Even sun lovers like succulents can burn and shrivel when suddenly exposed to the direct sunlight of May or June. After all the time and attention that you've lavished on them, most plants—especially baby plants—need special care when being introduced to the outside world.

The process of moving plants from inside to outside should not begin until the temperature outdoors is above 55°F. Cloudy days are far better for hardening off (acclimating) than sunny days, and shade lovers such as coleuses, ferns, and begonias should never be exposed to direct sun.

Two steps are involved in conditioning indoor plants for a successful vacation outdoors. The first step is to put them outside, and the second step is to bring them back inside. That's all there is to it, but you'll be lifting lots of pots back and forth before your plants can safely stay outside for a warm-weather break.

Once the right day arrives (at least 55°F and, hopefully, a bit cloudy but not windy), put as many of your plants as possible outside for about one hour. Then bring them back inside. Increase the outdoor time each day by one hour, and for sun-loving plants like geraniums, slowly move them into direct light at the same pace. When nighttime temperatures stay reliably above 55°F, your plants can camp out indefinitely. Just remember that during violent rain or hail storms, plants may need protection to keep their leaves from being shredded.

If you don't have access to a suitable outdoor warm-weather space for plants, don't worry as long as you have a window or two that can be opened for air circulation. You and your plants will lead a healthier life if air-conditioning is used only during the most unbearable heat—all living things benefit from time in fresh air.

> RIGHT *These baby plants will require at least one week to harden off before becoming outdoor residents.*

cana is also easy to increase, but not by way of its dangerously thorny leaves. The agave constantly creates suckers, sometimes affectionately called "pups," around its base. When these little agaves are about three inches tall, use a sharp knife to poke into the soil and cut the root that connects the pup to the big plant. Leave the pup on a plate to dry for a couple of days, and then pot it up in a small container of very sandy soil. Plant it just deep enough so that it stands up by itself, and water very sparingly. Stiff, prickly new leaves will begin to sprout in about one month.

❧ ABOVE *Small coleus cuttings enjoy the moist atmosphere trapped under inverted artichoke heart jars. The nearby radiator provides the extra warmth needed for successful winter growth.*

Sticks and Twigs. Most woody plants are not easily propagated, with the happy exception of the willows. If you force long streams of bright yellow weeping willow stems during the winter, you can easily end up with several new baby trees next year. By the time that beautiful pale green leaves appear along the stems, long white roots will have sprouted from the submerged wood. Bearing in mind that willows really love moist soil, place these rooted stems in very sandy soil in a clay pot with a saucer underneath. Keep the soil in the pot very wet, in this instance allowing the saucer to sit full of water. Place the new willow trees out of direct sun, and gradually introduce them to outdoor life by placing the pots in a shady spot when the weather stays above 55°F at night. Water them well all summer, and transplant into the ground in autumn. Forced pussy willows also root in water very easily and will make handsome shrubs if they receive the same treatment as weeping willows.

Another type of tree that you may have fun trying to start indoors is the oak. There are more than 450 species in the genus *Quercus,* with some evergreen oaks suited to warmer climates

~ RIGHT *Acorns gathered in autumn will sprout in water and can eventually be transplanted outdoors. These took about one month to sprout.*

and other deciduous types happy in colder weather. Everyone knows that mighty oaks spring from humble acorns, but not many people realize that these nuts can be gathered off the ground in autumn and easily sprouted in a dish of water on a north-facing windowsill.

THE ESSENTIALS OF CODDLING

Baby plants like to be warm. Old-fashioned radiators come in handy, but if you don't have those iron clunkers, figure out the warmest spots you do have and make a little nursery. Be sure to protect any delicate surfaces from the water that's going to be dripped around, because you're going to have to mist several times a day. The spot also needs to be out of direct sunlight (a no-brainer if you are rooting coleus, begonia, and other shade-loving plants) because new plants sunburn quite easily.

Begonias with fibrous roots are easy plants to propagate and benefit beautifully from TLC. Break off a leaf from the main plant right where it joins the stem. Place the leaf stem in a small jar of water so that the leaf is out of the water but as much of the stem as possible is submerged. Invert a glass bowl over the jar and the leaf to make a miniature homemade terrarium. This will give the begonia the extra moisture it loves. Place the entire show in a warm, shady spot, and roots will emerge from the bottom of the stem in about a month. When these roots are several inches long, pot the leaf in soil in a small clay pot (according to the coleus directions on page 139), water well, and replace under glass. In about a month new leaves will sprout underneath the big leaf, and a new begonia plant is born. At this stage you can cut off the old begonia leaf and remove the glass covering, making sure your new plant happily stays in its preferred warm, moist atmosphere.

Propagation Primer

The Mighty Oak

Although collecting flowers and branches from the wild is seldom condoned, picking up several acorns off the ground is harmless. Oak trees produce hundreds of acorns every autumn, but only one or two remain viable long enough to become oak trees. Many acorns fail to produce trees because they're eaten by wild animals such as squirrels and deer, and some just fall on inhospitable places like ponds, sidewalks, or lawns. Don't, however, pick acorns off trees—it's better to wait until they ripen and drop to the ground. Generally, this occurs sometime in late autumn or early winter.

To begin your oak tree indoors, you'll need to sprout these hard little nuts. Simply fill a shallow bowl with pebbles and add water up to the top of

the rocks. Place the acorns among the rocks and make sure that the water always stays high enough to keep the bottom of the acorns wet. After a few weeks, watch as the bottom of each acorn slowly cracks open and extends a thick white root into the water. Soon after, another crack (in the top) will yield a small twiggish stem that sprouts tiny, recognizable oak leaves.

Now comes the difficult part. When the sprouted acorn has at least two leaves, it's time to put it into soil. Fill a deep plastic pot with potting soil mixed with a cup of sand. Transplant this baby tree into a deep pot of soil, taking care not to bend or damage the long taproot, and keep well watered. Move your potted baby oaks into a cold frame, garage, or the protected place you use for chilling forced bulbs, and store them for the winter. Don't worry if the leaves fall off because many oaks lose their leaves in winter anyway. Next spring, you can transplant into the garden those that resprout with new leaves, once again taking care not to injure the long taproot.

If you have no garden for planting out, an outdoor gardening friend may be very grateful to receive free baby trees and shrubs. That friend will also probably recall your gifts next winter when you want to clip a few more branches for forcing (especially if you are as generous with hints as you are with plants).

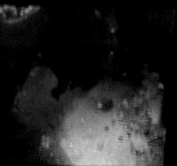
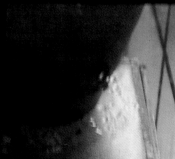

Baby coleus plants also like the extra protection of glass. If they are very small, an inverted big jar or inexpensive wide-mouthed glass vase will do the trick. The idea is to keep the moisture level up, so don't worry if water forms on the inside of the glass.

Gardening is truly learned only by active participation, and the wise enthusiast quickly sees that success is merely a fascinating process. If you grow one yellow crocus or coddle one new plant, it's possible to experience the undeniable natural pull that links people to plants. So get going—and get growing.

THE JOURNEY BEGINS

There is no such thing as 100 percent success in the realm of plant propagation. Likewise, some of your hardy bulbs will refuse to bloom, and your tender bulbs will sulk occasionally and suffer from lackluster growth. Even the most gorgeous, healthy houseplant will up and die suddenly, or a forced peach branch will blast into little brown knots. Experienced gardeners who take these developments in stride are among the happiest people you'll every meet.

✎ LEFT *Richard Felber coddles his begonia cuttings in a tabletop greenhouse.*

RESOURCE GUIDE

The sources listed here have been used by the author over many years. All are highly recommended and reliable, and they guarantee their products. Please mention this book when ordering.

Chapter One: HARDY BULBS

BEAUTY FROM BULBS
JOHN SCHEEPERS
23 TULIP DRIVE
BANTAM, CT 06750
TELEPHONE: (860) 567-0838
FAX: (860) 567-5323
www.johnscheepers.com
A great color catalog; minimum $25.

BRENT AND BECKY'S BULBS
7463 HEATH TRAIL
GLOUCESTER, VA 23061
TELEPHONE: (804) 693-3966
TOLL-FREE: (877) 661-2852
FAX: (804) 693-9436
www.brentandbeckysbulbs.com
Family-run business with an enormous selection and personal service.

OLD HOUSE GARDENS
SCOTT KUNST
536 THIRD ST.
ANN ARBOR, MI 48103-4957
TELEPHONE: (734) 995-1486
FAX: (734) 995-1687

www.oldhousegardens.com
Specialists in heirloom bulbs; a fascinating catalog ($2) and personal service.

MCCLURE & ZIMMERMAN
108 W. WINNEBAGO STREET
PO BOX 368
FRIESLAND, WI 53935-0368
TELEPHONE: (800) 883-6998
FAX: (800) 692-5864
www.mzbulb.com
Flower bulb brokers who carry a large selection; efficient service.

SMITH & HAWKEN
117 E. STRAWBERRY DRIVE
MILL VALLEY, CA 94941
TELEPHONE: (800) 981-9888
FAX: (606) 727-1166
www.smithandhawken.com
Prechilled, potted hardy bulbs ready to bloom; a good selection of pots and other containers.

VAN BOURGONDIEN
245 FARMINGDALE ROAD
PO BOX 1000
BABYLON, NY 11202
TELEPHONE: (800) 622-9997
FAX: (516) 669-1228
www.dutchbulbs.com
A good selection of hardy bulbs and good service.

VAN ENGELEN
23 TULIP DRIVE
BANTAM, CT 06750
TELEPHONE: (860) 567-8734
FAX: (860) 567-5323
www.vanengelen.com
Large selection and volume discounts; $50 minimum.

WHITE FLOWER FARM
30 IRENE STREET
TORRINGTON, CT 06790-6688
TELEPHONE: (800) 255-2852
FAX: (800) 420-2852
www.whiteflowerfarm.com
Efficient, friendly service and a wide selection of hardy bulbs.

Chapter Two: TENDER BULBS

BEAUTY FROM BULBS
(SEE INFORMATION ABOVE.)
A limited selection of tender bulbs; beautiful color catalog.

BRENT & BECKY'S BULBS
(SEE ADDRESS ABOVE.)
Separate catalog for tender bulbs and many other summer bloomers.

JIM DUGGAN FLOWER NURSERY
1452 SANTA FE DRIVE
ENCINITAS, CA 92024
TELEPHONE: (760) 943-1658
www.thebulbman.com
A small company offering good service and a fine collection of tender South African bulbs.

GREENLADY GARDENS
1415 EUCALYPTUS DRIVE
SAN FRANCISCO, CA 94132
TELEPHONE: (415) 753-3332
TOLL-FREE: (800) 841-1377
FAX: (415) 665-3308
A wide selection of tender bulbs; personal service.

SMITH & HAWKEN
(SEE ADDRESS ABOVE.)
A selection of tenders, paperwhites, and amaryllis.

VAN BOURGONDIEN
(SEE ADDRESS ABOVE.)
A limited selection of tenders, good catalog photos, and good service.

Chapter Three: HOUSEPLANTS

CARLSON'S GREENHOUSES
EAST MOUNTAIN ROAD SOUTH
COLD SPRING, NY 10516
TELEPHONE: (914) 265-9307
The author's favorite source for many tender bulbs and houseplants. Victor Carlson and his daughter Diane Phillips generously share their knowledge with visitors. No mail-order.

LOGEE'S GREENHOUSES
141 NORTH STREET
DANIELSON, CT 06239
TELEPHONE: (860) 774-8038
FAX: (860) 774-9932
www.logees.com
A multi-generation family business with excellent selection and good service.

SMITH & HAWKEN
(SEE ADDRESS ABOVE.)
A good selection of plants especially suitable for gifts.

WHITE FLOWER FARM
(SEE ADDRESS ABOVE.)
A selection of winter-blooming plants.

Individual Artisans

DEAN ANDERSON
CUSTOM IRONWORKS
TELEPHONE: (800) 823-5344
FAX: (914) 565-3539
Iron tutuers, trellises, slate-topped plant tables, and ornamental ironworks, made-to-order or from their catalog.

STACEY FARLEY
FARLEY TILES
TELEPHONE: (914) 736-5671
FAX: (914) 736-5904
Handmade tiles and tile murals, tiled trays, and bas-relief tilework.

NILS G. KULLESEID
STONE CARVER AND LETTER CUTTER
TELEPHONE: (914) 255-5346
FAX: (914) 736-1759
susnils@hvi.net
Custom stone carving and garden objects from a classically trained artist.